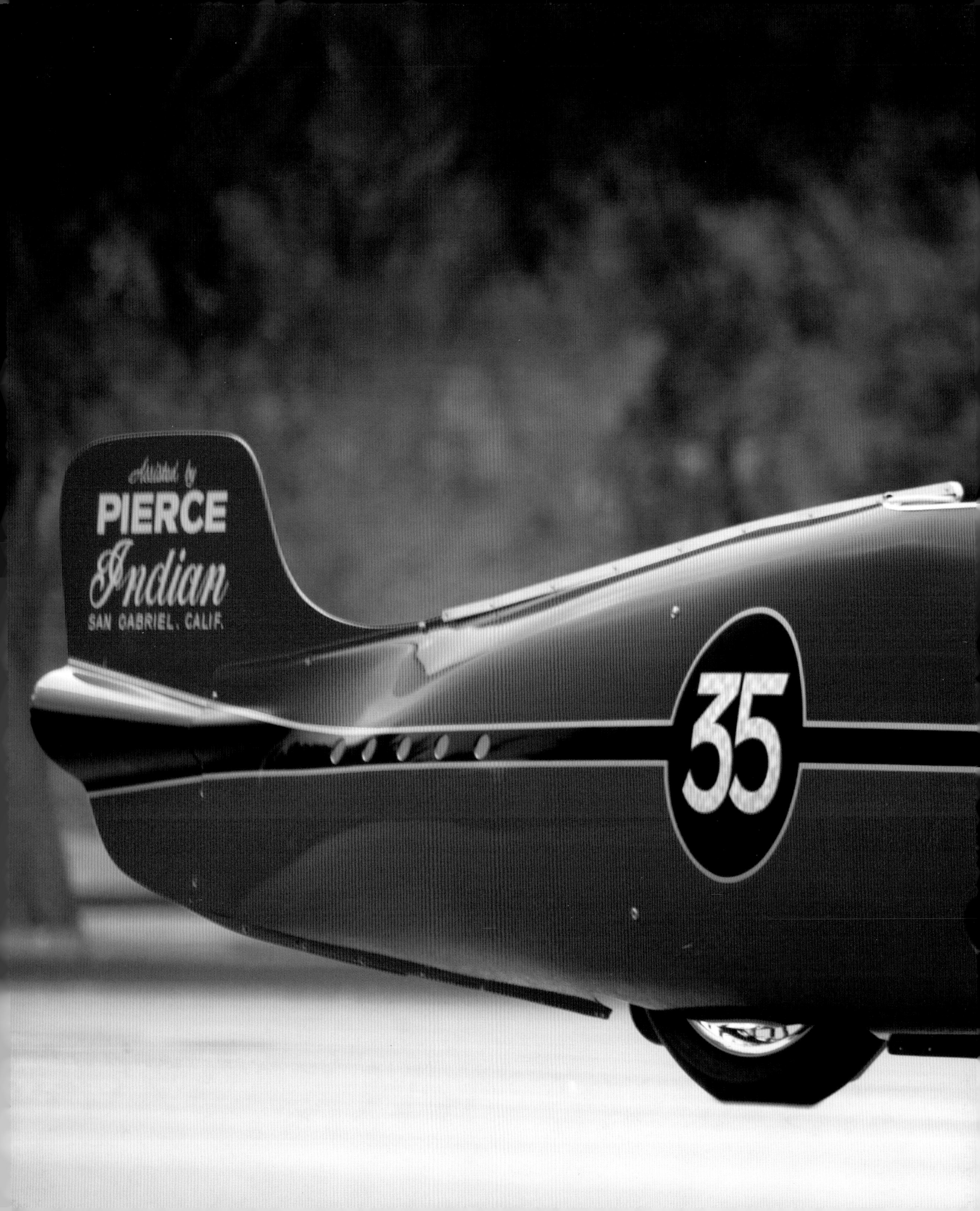
Assisted by
PIERCE
Indian
SAN GABRIEL, CALIF.
35

LEGENDARY MOTORCYCLES

The Stories and Bikes Made Famous by Elvis, Peter Fonda, Kenny Roberts, and Other Motorcycling Greats

MUNRO *Special*

Indian

1920 *Scout*

By Basem Wasef
FOREWORD BY JAY LENO

m motorbooks

Dedication

For Anna, the love of my life.

First published in 2007 by MBI Publishing Company and Motorbooks, an imprint of MBI Publishing Company, 400 1st Avenue North, Suite 300, Minneapolis, MN 55401 USA

Motorbooks titles are also available at discounts in bulk quantity for industrial or sales-promotional use. For details write to Special Sales Manager at MBI Publishing Company, 400 1st Avenue North, Suite 300, Minneapolis, MN 55401 USA.

To find out more about our books, join us online at www.motorbooks.com.

Editor: Lindsay Hitch
Designer: Christopher Fayers
Cover design: Tom Heffron

Printed in China

Library of Congress Cataloging-in-Publication Data

Wasef, Basem, 1972-
    Legendary motorcycles: the stories and bikes made famous by Elvis, Peter Fonda, Kenny Roberts, and other motorcycling greats / Basem Wasef.
        p. cm.
    Includes index.
    ISBN-13: 978-0-7603-3070-8 (hardbound w/ jacket)
    1. Antique and classic motorcycles. 2. Stage props. 3. Celebrities--Collectibles. I. Title.
TL444.2.W37 2007
629.227'50922—dc22

                                    2007009290

All photographs by Basem Wasef unless otherwise noted.

On the front cover: Captain America's stars-and-stripes peanut tank was painted by pinstriper Von Dutch; owner John Parham's tank echoes the original design.

On the spine: A rider's view of Dick Mann's Matchless G50 TT.

On the frontispiece: Lightweight but strong carbon fiber was incorporated liberally throughout the Britten V-1000, including the swingarm and the wheels.

On the title pages: The Munro Special is currently owned by the Hensley family.

On the back cover: Steve McQueen rides his TR6SC Triumph through the streets of London prior to competing in the International Six Days Trials. *Sean Kelly*

CONTENTS

FOREWORD BY JAY LENO 7

ACKNOWLEDGMENTS 8

INTRODUCTION 10

1 JAMES DEAN'S FIRST AND LAST BIKES
—A FASCINATION WITH SPEED 12

2 KENNY ROBERTS' YAMAHA TZ750 DIRT TRACKER
—"THEY DON'T PAY ME ENOUGH TO RIDE THAT THING." 20

3 T. C. CHRISTENSEN'S HOGSLAYER
—THE NORTON WITH AN INSATIABLE APPETITE FOR HARLEYS 26

4 ROLLIE FREE'S JOHN EDGAR LIGHTNING
—THE BATHING SUIT BIKE 32

5 MERT LAWWILL'S NO. 1 1969 HARLEY-DAVIDSON KR750
—FINAL VICTORY FOR A BATTLE-AX 40

6 EASY RIDER'S CAPTAIN AMERICA
—A STAR-SPANGLED AMERICAN ICON 46

7 DICK MANN'S BSA GOLD STAR AND MATCHLESS G50 TT
—THE TOOLS OF THE TRADE 52

8 FREDDIE SPENCER'S 1985 DOUBLE CHAMPIONSHIP HONDA GP BIKES
—LIVING THE IMPOSSIBLE DREAM 58

9 CRAIG VETTER'S MYSTERY SHIP
—THE CHILDHOOD FANTASY BIKE 66

10 CAL RAYBORN'S NO. 3 HARLEY-DAVIDSON XR750
—A TRANSATLANTIC SENSATION 72

11 WAYNE RAINEY'S 1983 KAWASAKI SUPERBIKE
—THE AIR-COOLED UNDERDOG 78

12 COLIN EDWARDS' YAMAHA TZ250D
—THE BIKE THAT LAUNCHED A CAREER .84

13 LEO PAYNE'S TURNIP EATER

—THE 200-MILE-PER-HOUR HOG 88

14 T. E. LAWRENCE'S BROUGH SUPERIOR SS100

—LAWRENCE OF ARABIA'S LAST RIDE 94

15 ELVIS PRESLEY'S HARLEY-DAVIDSON ELECTRA-GLIDE

—A RIDE FIT FOR THE KING 100

16 JOHN BRITTEN'S BRITTEN V-1000

—THE MODERN MASTERPIECE 106

17 EVEL KNIEVEL'S HARLEY-DAVIDSONS

—THE ORIGINAL DAREDEVIL'S CHARIOTS OF CHOICE 112

18 VON DUTCH'S ORIGINALS

—CUSTOMIZING AS AN ART FORM .118

19 MICHAEL JORDAN'S AMA RACING CONTENDERS

—A BASKETBALL LEGEND'S PASSION FOR RACING 126

20 MIKE HAILWOOD'S DUCATI COMEBACK BIKES

—A HERO'S RETURNS TO THE ISLE OF MAN 132

21 MARTY DICKERSON'S BLUE BIKE

—BONNEVILLE'S IRRESISTIBLE ALLURE 136

22 BURT MUNRO'S MUNRO SPECIAL

—THE WORLD'S FASTEST INDIAN .142

23 RENZO PASOLINI'S HARLEY-DAVIDSON XR750

—ITALO-AMERICAN CHEMISTRY 152

24 PHIL READ'S MV AGUSTA GP BIKES

—MV'S LAST HURRAH 156

25 ROBERT PIRSIG'S HONDA CB77 SUPERHAWK

—INSPIRING ZEN AND THE ART OF MOTORCYCLE MAINTENANCE . . .162

26 STEVE MCQUEEN'S GREAT ESCAPES

—RIDING WITH THE KING OF COOL 166

TIMELINE 174

INDEX 176

FOREWORD

A while back, a rumor circulated that I had bought Elvis' Harley for a million bucks. Now, while I enjoy a sizable collection of unusual motorcycles, I love old bikes because of what makes them unique, whether it's oddball technology, neat design, or craftsmanship that you just don't see anymore. Not to say that there aren't great bikes that also happened to have famous butts sit on them (like Elvis or James Dean), or bikes that became legendary because they were so rare and radically designed (like the Britten V-1000)—or even bikes that became famous for killing their owner (think of poor old T. E. Lawrence)—but if I put something in my garage, I want to be able to cruise around town on it and not have to worry about destroying the personal possession of somebody loved and adored by millions. If I go down on my Velocette Thruxton, I'll at least have the comfort of knowing that my mistake (or, more likely, the mistake of the idiot in the SUV who cut me off while talking on a cell phone) won't disturb history too much.

Motorcycles are made to be ridden. As good as they might look on display, they really look better at speed; that's what they're intended for. I've ridden many of the same kinds of motorcycles featured in this book, and believe me, they're more fun to ride than to just look at. That being said, when I was a kid, I used to wonder how people could go into an art museum and stare at a painting for a half hour. It never made sense to me, but now it does. Oftentimes, I'll go into my garage, pull up a chair, and just look at the Vincent Black Shadow. To me, that's one of the prettiest motorcycles ever made. I've said many times that I can't trust a motorcycle I can't see through, and with a Vincent Black Shadow, there are just so many places for your eye to fall.

On the other hand, there's a lot of emotion connected to a handful of exceptional motorcycles, a few machines that not only represent a certain place or person but also capture a moment in time. Whether it's Evel Knievel's wipeout at Wembley Stadium or the image of Peter Fonda riding *Captain America* across the country in *Easy Rider*, the bikes in *Legendary Motorcycles* have their own magic . . . something that gives them a special place in history.

—Jay Leno, March 2007

ACKNOWLEDGMENTS

First on the long list of people who deserve my extended gratitude is Zack Miller, whose passion for bikes led him to champion *Legendary Motorcycles.* He has been a great co-conspirator in this project, and his intimate knowledge of and enthusiasm for the subject has been a tremendous asset. I am indebted to Randy Leffingwell for introducing me to Zack and for being so willing to share his extensive experience and expertise. Editor Lee Klancher demystified the publishing process and was an excellent sounding board. My ongoing dialogue with Lindsay Hitch was always a pleasure and she efficiently streamlined the flow of photos, words, and ideas. The entire MBI team brought everything together wonderfully.

My wife, Anna, was selfless, tireless, and an ebullient ambassador of good will. Her assistance ranged from persuading reluctant owners to participate to shooing away chickens while I shot bikes, and most importantly, helping edit the photos and text; I couldn't have done it without her.

In somewhat chronological order: Thanks to Elke Martin, who connected me to Mark Mederski at the AMA Motorcycle Museum Hall of Fame in Pickerington, Ohio, the first stop on our cross-country drive. Mark was incredibly generous with his time and energy, and gave great insight into our project. At his museum, we shot bikes raced by Dick Mann, who is a disarmingly humble man of few words; Ed Youngblood, author of *Mann of His Time,* assisted in recounting his incredible career. Similarly, I was refreshed by Mert Lawwill's positive attitude and generosity with historical photos, and the assistance of his son, Joe. Craig Vetter offered a fascinating perspective on his *Mystery Ship* and the future of fuel-efficient vehicles. In Fairmount, Indiana, Marcus Winslow, Jr. and his son, Coy, went to great lengths to enable the photography of James Dean's first and last bikes, and Marcus' memories of Jimmy offered an evocative insight into the life and passions of the short-lived star. T. C. Christensen's recollections of his racing career transported us to another time and place, and it was a pleasure to see him still blazing the streets of Kenosha, Wisconsin, on his Norton.

Jeff Carstensen and John Parham were instrumental in the photography of the bikes at the National Motorcycle Museum in Anamosa, Iowa. Thanks to Ted Rieniets, I was fortunate enough to find Dave Geisler Sr., my new friend by the side of the road who, along with his son, Dave Jr., facilitated my photography of Elvis' Harley at the Pioneer Auto Show in Murdo, South Dakota. In Butte, Montana, Krystal Knievel was pivotal in providing access to and photos of her husband, Evel Knievel, whose tenacity and refusal to back down is inspiring. The owner of the Brough Superior SS100 that killed T. E. Lawrence, who wishes not to be named, volunteered not only historical photographs but also countless detailed facts that aided the Lawrence chapter immensely. Photographer Jim Mann essentially saved me a trip to the U.K. I owe you one, Jim.

Brian Slark, Joe Bruton, and Ken Brogan of the Barber Vintage Motorsports Museum in Birmingham, Alabama, tended to my photographic and informational needs, while Lee Woehle assisted with a great deal of research. Ken Abbott made inside information and photography of Michael Jordan's AMA race bikes available, and Tom Halverson was a godsend arranging my interview with the easygoing Colin Edwards before he jetted off to Qatar for MotoGP testing. Gregg Kearns kindly connected me to "Fast Freddie,". Jon Seidel of American Honda deftly coordinated photography of Freddie Spencer's 500cc GP bike before it was shipped back to Japan. Freddie Spencer and his lovely wife, Cheleé, proved that even if you move out to the desert, you can bring that famous southern hospitality with you.

I greatly appreciated Herb Harris, not only for putting me up in his charming Austin, Texas, guest house, but also for his detailed stories, the access to his treasure trove of historical documents and photographs, and his physical efforts to load up and move the *John Edgar Lightning* and the *Blue Bike* one incredibly hot, humid September day. Marty Dickerson's energy, vivacity, and lust for life are infectious. He is inspirational, not only for sharing adventures with Rollie Free and Burt Munro, but for continuing to ride at the age of 80.

Virgil Elings, the owner of the Solvang Vintage Motorcycle Museum, offered plenty of wry observations and wit regarding his Britten V-1000. Up in Morro Bay, California, Stephen Wright competed with Virgil for the driest, wryest commentary; Stephen's a fountain of razor-sharp information about his Kenny Roberts Yahama TZ750, as well as a number of other bikes. Tom Hensley and Claudia Hoard graciously hosted us at their Los Osos home, and Tom's stories about his brother Dean and his generous access to the *Munro Special* was exceptional.

The incredibly laid-back Daniel Schoenewald is the enthusiast's enthusiast, and it's always a pleasure to talk bikes with him at his Camarillo, California, home. Bettina Chandler graciously arranged for photography of the 1926 Cleveland Fowler Four once owned by Steve McQueen and Otis Chandler. During the shoot, which took place in Oxnard, California, Stuart Munger regaled us with many humorous motorcycle anecdotes. Al Quattrocchi's company, Tornado Design, published a wonderfully visual book titled *The Art of Von Dutch*, and was kind enough to introduce me to Bird Betts, who elucidated the enigmatic figure of his uncle, Von Dutch.

Phil Read colorfully illuminated the final throes of MV Agusta's magnificent Grand Prix reign, and John Sutherland's memories of Robert Pirsig added dimension to the ride that inspired *Zen and the Art of Motorcycle Maintenance*. Ollie Foran, the current owner of the BMW R60/2 that Sutherland rode, offered a unique perspective on the bike, and Professor Henry Gurr shared beautiful photos from the famous ride. His website is required reading for any fan of the book: http://ww2.usca.edu/ResearchProjects/ProfessorGurr/. Loren Roberts generously assisted in the photo clearance process for several chapters.

Thanks to the inimitable Bud Ekins for his revealing stories on everything from the making of *Easy Rider* and *The Great Escape* to life with Steve McQueen and Von Dutch. Sean Kelly's prescient connoisseurship of style is manifest in his Johnson Motors stores and clothing line, and he has gone to great lengths to keep the McQueen flame alive. Levi Medina at Johnson Motors offered encouragement and assistance, and John Pera provided plenty of ideas and information regarding many of the bikes featured here. Mike and Margaret Wilson are living proof of motorcycling's rejuvenating effects on both relationships and worldviews, and Don Emde provided a vivid account of the 1972 Transatlantic Match Races, not to mention many historical photographs from his archives.

My parents and family have been exceptionally supportive—despite their abject fear of motorcycles—though I suppose it filled them with a certain delight when I reminded them that the subjects of this book are bikes I wouldn't get to ride. Ernesto Cuevas' peerless Photoshopping skills and superb taste were great assets. Regarding Jay Leno, I can't say enough good things about his warmth, accessibility, and professionalism. Jay's about as down to earth as it gets, a bona fide gearhead whose genuine excitement about bikes and cars is contagious. Finally and most importantly, I thank God for the opportunity to celebrate these people and their achievements through my work.

INTRODUCTION

The idea for *Legendary Motorcycles* grew out of a telephone conversation with Zack Miller, and like many great concepts, it developed from one simple thought: "What if we made a book about the most historically significant motorcycles ever, *the* bikes that became famous?" It was an intriguing proposition, and before long, lists were compiled and revised, investigative phone calls were placed, and the book started to take shape. Some bikes made their locations readily available, while others appeared to be lost forever... for instance, what ever happened to Hunter S. Thompson's motorcycles or the Norton Che Guevera rode throughout South America? The beauty of the hunt came not from the information I expected to receive, but from tangential clues and unexpected leads that emerged from the unlikeliest of sources. With my list narrowing and a map of the United States dotted with destinations, I plotted a zigzagging course across the country that would occupy me for most of the summer of 2006.

Because adventure loves company, I scheduled the trip so it included my wife, Anna, who, for-tuitously, was costume designing a film just outside of Atlanta, Georgia. I had always wanted to write a book, but the project also became an opportunity to fulfill another dream: purchasing and driving a sports car cross-country, an element which came together when I bought a 1983 Porsche 911 SC from Orlando, Florida.

By mid-July, we set out for the open road, our luggage, photography equipment, and rice cooker crammed into the small, slate-blue 911. With much of the same unpredictability as the research process, doors swung unexpectedly open and closed, forcing us to shift routes and change schedules at the last moment. Shooting Elvis' bikes at Graceland, for instance, became a logistical and budgetary impossibility, but an unexpected tip led us to a little-known Elvis bike that resides in Murdo, South Dakota. It was our first cross-country drive, and falling into the rhythm of life on the road was surprisingly easy; as we checked bikes off our list and generally lived by the seat of our nomadic pants, the details of the book became increasingly clear. We decided to avoid major inter-states and become intimately acquainted with the forgotten small towns of America. All the while, the Porsche was, much to our relief, surprisingly reliable. It also served as a great conversation starter amongst the Ford and Chevy crowds, some of whom were taken aback by its alien shape.

While traversing the shifting landscapes of middle America, there was something wonderfully gratifying about photographing each bike in an environment that suited its personality. For instance, removing James Dean's Triumph from its massive Lucite display case at the Fairmount His-torical Museum required enlisting the town's volunteer fire department, but using Dean's childhood home as a backdrop allowed for a rare photographic opportunity to juxtapose the last bike he owned with the rural innocence of his early surroundings. On the other hand, taking T. C. Christensen's massive triple-engined Norton *Hogslayer* outside of his Kenosha, Wisconsin, workshop would have been even more labor-intensive, so we shot it perched on Campbell's soup crates inside the garage, which turned out to be the perfect way to capture the bike's homegrown quirkiness.

Throughout the making of *Legendary Motorcycles*, we were treated to an intimate glimpse at the passionate, lifelong relationships people form with bikes. Following an afternoon of photography, we often indulged in the afterglow of the hot summer sun by sipping beer and listening to stories from these living legends. Our experiences took on an almost surreal quality, with relaxed conversations melting into the quiet of evening. There was an elegant simplicity to the goals of our trip; we would photograph and interview, maximizing the late afternoon light and the generosity of our subjects, and then plan the route ahead and repeat the process.

In between destinations, we used our National Park passes, buffering our motorcycle-related stops with the stunning natural beauty of Yellowstone, Devil's Tower, the Badlands, Bryce, and Zion. As cornfields and prairie dissolved into the rugged landscape of the west, we became struck with that unmistakable longing for home. After finally reacquainting ourselves with Los Angeles, several subjects in California put us on the road again, and I made one more cross-country trip, this time by air, to southern destinations we missed the first time around.

The process of photographing and writing *Legendary Motorcycles* was an unforgettable experience, one that unfolded organically from one simple question. If you enjoy this book nearly as much as I enjoyed making it, I would consider my efforts a success.

1

JAMES DEAN'S
FIRST AND LAST BIKES

A Fascination with Speed

James Dean's love affair with speed may have been immortalized by his death in a Porsche 550 Spyder, but it began on two wheels almost a decade earlier. At the age of 15, Dean was given his first real motorcycle —a 1947 CZ 125-cc—by his uncle and guardian, Marcus Winslow. The CZ was a no-nonsense, Czech-manufactured bike, but it imbued Dean with a sense of freedom inaccessible to most kids of his age in the farming town of Fairmount, Indiana.

Replacing his Whizzer, which was essentially a small motor attached to a bicycle, the CZ became an indelible part of Dean's budding personality. In 1948, the school principal assigned students to write about themselves, and Dean wrote proudly, "My hobby, or what I do in my spare time, is motor cycle. I know a lot about them mechanically and I love to ride. I have been in a few races, and I have done well. I own a small cycle myself."

Opposite: James Dean enjoys a rare static moment on his Triumph.
Courtesy of JamesDeanGallery.com

James Dean's A model CZ 125-cc was tricky to operate. The bike required three hands— one for the throttle, one for the clutch, and another for the tank-mounted shifter.

"Jimmy was really a pistol," explains Marvin Carter, who sold him the 4-horsepower bike that was capable of 50 miles per hour. "They called him 'One Speed Dean.' One speed: wide open." Dean raced the bike on an improvised track behind Carter's motorcycle shop and quickly developed a reputation for mischief. "It was a real noisy cycle. Sounded like a bumblebee," recalls Dean's cousin, Marcus Winslow Jr., whom Dean treated like a brother. "He would go over to the crossroads, turn that little Czech motorcycle around, stick his feet straight out the back, and ride it as fast as it would go. My mom used to get aggravated with him for riding like that." Dean's prone posture was probably inspired by Rollie Free, who broke the motorcycle land speed record in 1948 by stripping to his underwear and lying on the gas tank.

The CZ was not only Dean's source of adrenaline; it also allowed him moments of introspection. "He would often ride it to the homestead and meditate on it. He seemed to derive a certain amount of comfort from it," Marvin Carter explains. After high school, Dean decided to move to Los Angeles, and the graduation gift of a trip to the Indianapolis 500 cemented his fascination with racing. "It's the only time I feel whole," he would later say of the sport.

After dropping out of UCLA and landing several bit parts in television and commercials, Dean moved to New York City to immerse himself in acting. He visited Fairmount over the holidays

The 1947 CZ 125-cc was purchased from the Indian dealership seen behind it, which is now an empty building.

and traded in his CZ for a more exotic Royal Enfield 500-cc vertical twin, which he was warned had a newly rebuilt engine that needed to be broken in gently. Dean insisted on bundling up and riding back to New York in the middle of winter, and he made it to the Pennsylvania turnpike before burning an exhaust valve.

While the Enfield's parts were being shipped, Dean fell hard for a maroon and gold striped 1952 Indian Warrior TT that was on display in the showroom of the shop where his bike was being repaired. He negotiated a $300 trade-in value for the Enfield and produced an additional $400 by having his New York agent forward him acting checks. His serial weakness for cars and motorcycles would grow as his career progressed, and he continued to indulge in faster, more beautiful machines.

Back in New York, Dean stored his motorcycle at the Greenwich Village garage where Steve McQueen worked as a part-time motorcycle mechanic, and the two would bond over their love of bikes. When director Elia Kazan considered Dean for a role in the film *East of Eden*, he reluctantly agreed to a harrowing ride down Broadway on the Indian. Though Kazan would later say of Dean that "conversation was not his gift," something about his vitality resonated with Kazan, and Dean landed the part that would launch his career. A few months later in Los Angeles, Dean signed a nine-picture deal with Warner Bros., and using part of his advance from *East of Eden,* he purchased a used red MG TD and a shell blue 1955 Triumph T110.

Three days after the filming of *East of Eden* wrapped, Dean traded his T110 for a 1955 Triumph TR5 Trophy, VIN TR559196, at Ted Evans Motorcycles in Culver City. Like his first Triumph, the Trophy was shell blue, but Dean made the bike his own through a number of modifications, including the installation of upright handlebars by Flanders, the removal of the muffler in favor of louder, straight pipes, and the installation of an older, 6T-style rider seat. He also flipped the passenger seat backward, the same way Marlon Brando did on his 1950 Triumph 6T in *The Wild One*.

Between the filming of *East of Eden* and his next film, *Rebel Without a Cause*, Dean became heartbroken when his relationship with Italian actress Pier Angeli ended. During her wedding to singer Vic Damone, Dean pulled up on his Triumph, waited for the couple to emerge from the church, and revved his engine defiantly from across the street before thundering away. Once again, the machine became an instrument of his expression.

Dean's rapidly escalating success gave him the means to enjoy more exotic machines; his MG was replaced with a white 1955 Porsche 356 Super Speedster. Unlike Elia Kazan, who discouraged Dean's reckless behavior, Nicholas Ray, the director of *Rebel Without a Cause*, embraced the actor's dangerous streak and allowed him to race his Porsche for the first time just days before photography commenced. Producer Mort Abrahams would later comment that Natalie Wood, Dean's co-star, "didn't quite know how to deal with this man who roared up on his motorbike every day. He could be alternately jolly, charming, and funny, then twenty minutes later off by himself 'sulking.' But he only *appeared* to be sulking; he was actually inside of himself." Whether Dean was method acting or genuinely moody, his distinctive style translated to on-screen charisma, and the line between fiction and reality often became blurred. Marcus Winslow Jr. comments, "It didn't seem like he was acting; it just seemed like Jimmy was up there, the way he walked, the way he carried himself." Indeed, if the painful vulnerability of Dean's dramatic characters were beautifully evoked on screen, they would soon become tragically realized in real life.

Going directly from *Rebel Without a Cause* to George Stevens' epic film *Giant,* Dean once again found himself working for a director who did not care for his vehicular shenanigans. Close to the end of the filming of *Giant,* Dean ironically shot a public service announcement for the National Safety Council in which he discouraged speeding on public roads, adding nonchalantly, "Take it easy driving. The life you might save might be mine."

Dean's Triumph parked in front of the house in which he grew up.

James Dean's final bike, his 1955 Triumph TR5 Trophy, resting on a hill near the Winslow residence in Fairmount, Indiana, where he grew up.

When he was liberated from the responsibilities of the film, Dean traded in his Speedster for a silver 1955 Porsche 550 Spyder. "When a man goes home at night," declared Dean, "the studio can't tell him not to do what he wants to do." During his last day on the picture, Dean showed off his new toy on the Warner Bros. lot and insisted that Stevens take a spin with him, since he was now free to do as he pleased. Stevens would later quote studio guards as saying, "You can never drive this car on the lot again; you're gonna kill a carpenter or an actor or somebody." "That," Stevens said, "was the last time I saw Jimmy."

Less than a week after the completion of *Giant,* Dean decided to participate in a race in Salinas, California. Because his Spyder had only 150 miles on the clock and needed to be broken in, he chose to drive it rather than tow it. Just before 6:00 p.m. on September 30, 1955, at the intersection of highways 466 and 41, Dean's Porsche collided with a 1950 Ford Custom Tudor, ejecting and seriously injuring Dean's passenger, mechanic Rolf Wütherich. Dean, trapped in the wreckage of the Porsche, died almost instantly. He was only 24. James Dean's 16-month career produced two Academy Award Best Actor nominations, legions of fans, and an enduring mystique that attracts a yearly pilgrimage to his hometown of Fairmount, Indiana, over 50 years later.

During the late 1980s, Marcus Winslow Jr., who grew up with Dean and was only 12 at the time of his death, went on a quest to locate Dean's last bike, his 1955 Triumph T5 Trophy. After Jimmy's death, his father, Winton Dean, advertised the motorcycle for sale in the *Los Angeles Times* without clarifying that it had belonged to the star. According to Winslow, one of the only potential buyers was a motorcycle courier who lost interest in the bike when she learned that it had knobby tires. Upon realizing the difficulty of selling the Triumph, Winton Dean sold it back to Ted Evans for around $400, about $50 less than what Jimmy had paid for it new. Through the help of Winslow's friend, who contacted Evans in order to track down its owner, the Triumph was traced to a man in Minnesota who had raced and heavily modified the bike. The serial number was verified against the number listed in James Dean's estate papers, and Winslow had the bike restored to its current, as-new condition—down to the backward-facing rear seat, the custom Flanders handlebars, and the straight-pipe exhaust.

After Dean had traded in his first bike, the 1947 CZ, for a Royal Enfield, the CZ was painted yellow, resold, and traded back in to Marvin Carter a few years later. Following Dean's death, Carter gave the bike to Marcus Winslow Sr., and the motorcycle spent some time on display at Paramount Studios in Los Angeles before returning to Fairmount. The bike remains in an unrestored state at the Fairmount Historical Museum, its yellow paint fading and revealing traces of black underneath.

A study in contrasts, Dean's 1947 CZ 125-cc and 1955 Triumph TR5 Trophy motorcycles represent not only his evolving sophistication and his growing appetite for speed, but also two sides of his famously complex and dynamic personality. Both rebellious and refined, authentic and beautiful, the bikes are as much a part of Dean's legacy as the countless photographs, the appearances in film and television, and the remaining artifacts of his singular personality.

James Dean's Triumph was restored by Marcus Winslow Jr. and his son in the 1980s.

Kenny Roberts

2

KENNY ROBERTS'

TZ750 DIRT TRACKER

*"They don't pay me enough
to ride that thing."*

Kenny Roberts' 1975 AMA Grand National season was shaping up to be a rough one. Primed by two Grand National Championships in 1973 and 1974, Roberts had every reason to expect continued success in 1975. However, his four-stroke, vertical-twin–powered Yamaha proved problematic, providing lackluster performance along with failing clutches, snapping chains, and electrical problems. Roberts was a remarkably skilled rider becoming a prisoner to inferior machinery, and he knew he could excel if only given the right equipment.

Despite his lagging performance, Roberts possessed enough self-preservation to resist a certain buzz that was escalating in the Yamaha camp. The controversial rumor began as a flight of fancy: While team mechanic Bob Work was transporting a new TZ750 road racer to Canada with teammate Steve Baker, he was struck with an unlikely idea—to transplant the explosively powerful TZ750 Grand Prix engine into a dirt

Opposite: Kenny Roberts negotiating a turn at the Indy Mile. *Bert Shepard*

tracker. Along the way to Canada, Work and Baker impulsively stopped at the shop of innovative frame builder Doug Schwerma in Hayward, California, where he took measurements and confirmed that the engine would indeed fit.

Such a Frankenstein job was not to be taken lightly, and when the concept of placing the outrageously powerful engine into the dirt tracker was debated, the voices of disapproval were loud. Nonetheless, the project moved forward, much to the reluctance of Roberts himself, who had perhaps the most to gain from a more competitive bike. Conversely, however, Roberts also had the most to lose. Considering the explosive power of the GP engine and its unproven chemistry with the dirt tracker frame, he had every reason to protest the experiment and fear the potentially deadly combination. A total of six TZ750 kits were built, and the initial experiences of racers Rick Hocking and Steve Baker were not promising. Because of the tremendous forces they were subjected to, swingarms bent and were subsequently braced, and wheel hub bearings loosened, which reinforced the opinion that the project was ill-conceived.

By mid-July, Roberts lost his points lead to Harley-Davidson's Gary Scott, and the downward slide continued. With V-twin-powered Harleys dominating the field, the argument for employing the TZ engine became stronger, and by the Indianapolis Mile event, builder Kel Carruthers had managed to cram the two-stroke TZ750 into Schwerma's frame. The chassis had a customized engine cradle that accommodated the TZ's large expansion chambers, and the swingarm was later lengthened by 1 inch to keep the front wheel from lifting.

Shortly before the Indianapolis race, Carruthers asked Roberts how fast he wanted to go at Indy. "About one thirty should be enough," replied Roberts, so Carruthers geared the bike to top out at approximately 130 miles per hour. The very same engine had been road raced at Laguna Seca the weekend before; apart from a top-end freshening, the engine retained essentially the same tune.

Race day—August 23, 1975—was the first time Roberts rode the bike, and despite the Herculean engine/chassis combination, practice laps were not promising. Carruthers had installed a kill button on the number three cylinder so Roberts could slow the engine down while he was going into turns (since two-strokes have, by nature, very little natural engine braking), but the undesired side effect was an almost instantaneous boost of roughly 30 horsepower when the button was released. So much power was transmitted to the rear wheel, in fact, that it frequently spun, making it difficult to effectively propel the bike out of turns. When it did hook up, the bike easily wheelied, making steering impossible. Roberts, disenchanted with what seemed like a doomed experiment, announced that two-strokes on large-scale dirt tracks would "ruin Mile racing like they have road racing." He complained to Schwerma and Carruthers: "What a piece of shit this thing is. It's the worst handling bike I ever rode. It won't steer. It won't turn. I can't ride it . . . I wish I had my twin here." In support of his complaints, the Harleys were producing considerably quicker practice laps, and come race time, things didn't look good for Roberts.

Starting from dead last, the TZ750 struggled to stay on the track. Rather than follow the rubber laid down by other bikes, which formed the racing line, Roberts maneuvered the beastly bike in wide arcs across the edge of the track, careening off the hay bales in order to not completely lose control. The brutal power of the TZ, however, had the potential to make up for time lost in the curves; its two-stroker pumped out an estimated 120 horsepower, rocketing it past the lesser-powered Harleys on straightaways.

The Yamaha TZ750 dirt tracker was photographed near Morro Bay, California. It was restored to the configuration in which it competed in its final race at the San Jose Mile.

Ken Maely's gas weld on the right footpeg helped Kel Carruthers confirm Stephen Wright's TZ750 as being the bike raced by Kenny Roberts in 1975. Another clue was the exhaust harness visible in the background.

Stephen Wright enlarged race photographs in order to accurately re-create period decals while restoring the TZ750.

As the laps wore away, Roberts worked his way through the field from the back of the pack, leveraging his unorthodox lines with hay bales and sheer determination (which was likely fueled by his anger toward the bike). In what would become quite possibly the most sensational final lap in motorcycle racing, Roberts did the unimaginable: coming out of the last turn of the 25th lap, far behind Harley riders Jay Springsteen and Corky Keener, Roberts managed to perfectly hook up the rear tire, slingshot the bike down the straight, and reel himself ever closer to the race leaders. During the last few laps of the race, Springsteen had held up his index finger to senior teammate Keener, who probably interpreted the gesture to mean that he could have first place if he wanted. However, Springsteen actually intended to communicate that Kenny Roberts, whose race number was 1, was rapidly approaching from behind. Barreling down the straight and just past Keener and Springsteen, Roberts won the race by half a bike length, cementing the controversy surrounding the dirt tracker with the GP engine.

After the race, Roberts credited the dirt cushion close to the hay bales as being the tool with which he made up for lost traction. "If I didn't go against the cushion, I couldn't have done what I did. I just kept going. It was still kind of scary. Whenever that thing did hook up with the racetrack, it was ungodly. Ungodly acceleration." Famously, Roberts then pointed to the bike and said, "They don't pay me enough to ride that thing," indicating its potentially lethal rough edges in one swoop of his fingertip. On the flight from Indianapolis, Schwerma—perhaps the bike's biggest proponent—asked Roberts, "Still jazzed, Kenny?" to which Roberts responded, "Doug, it's like I said. You're not the one that has to ride that thing."

Despite its stunning performance at Indianapolis, the TZ750 had poor results the only other times Roberts ran it—at Syracuse and San Jose. By the end of the season, the American Motorcyclist Association banned the bike with the telling support of Kel Carruthers, who had been responsible for bringing it to life. As the bike's unusual race history ended, its retirement opened an equally improbable new chapter. Two years after the 1975 season, Yamaha sent the TZ750 to England for a flat track promotional campaign where Peter Collins rode the bike—and though fitted with the largest possible rear sprocket, it was still difficult to control. Following the event, it was shipped to Yamaha's race headquarters in Amsterdam. Stripped of its engine, the rolling chassis had its exhaust taped to the frame, and because there was no use for the bike in Europe, Roberts' Grand Prix team manager Kenny Clark had it shipped back to the United States.

When a Japanese Yamaha liaison reviewed the inventory of retired race equipment in a California warehouse, he allowed Clark to keep the chassis. Though countless race bikes are routinely destroyed at a Santa Fe Springs, California, facility, the TZ escaped its date with the crusher because it fortuitously happened to be missing its motor. When restorer Stephen Wright was searching for parts for another bike, he called

Clark, who lived six miles away. Wright coincidentally asked, "By the way, what happened to the Roberts bike?" and Clark responded, "I've got it." Wright immediately negotiated to purchase the TZ750 and proceeded to restore it, using enlarged race photographs to ensure the accuracy of such details as period decals and wiring fitments.

While the TZ's original engine had been long separated from the bike, the AMA held on to a set of TZ750 engine cases, cylinders, and heads that were used to verify homologation. In the late 1970s, when AMA official Earl Flanders noticed that the powerplant had become obsolete, he shipped the parts to Clark, and they were sold to Wright along with the chassis.

A few unique points distinguish the Roberts TZ750 dirt tracker from the restored bike, among them a repair performed on the right footpeg, which was damaged when it hit a fence at San Jose. The peg was gas-welded at San Jose by metals expert Ken Maely, who only worked at West Coast races.

Wright, a bike restorer widely considered to be at the top of his field, displayed the bike at the Marlboro Roberts garage during the 1994 USGP, where Carruthers recognized the welded footpeg, a repaired brake arm, and the special mounting system he had built in order to tuck the exhaust tightly to the body. "It's the bike," he verified, and Roberts, upon seeing the link to his past, said, "I can't believe it, just can't believe it." More telling, though, was what Roberts told his father during a fishing trip two days after winning the Indy Mile. "I guess," Roberts reflected, "all things taken into consideration, that Indy race was one of my best rides ever."

Because flat-track events involve only left turns, two exhaust pipes were moved to the right of the bike for the San Jose Mile, leaving a small pipe on the left for improved clearance.

3

T. C. CHRISTENSEN'S

HOGSLAYER

The Norton with an Insatiable Appetite for Harleys

It took a certain type of personality to be attracted to foreign motorcycles in Kenosha, Wisconsin, during the 1950s. Riding anything but a Harley placed a person in a fundamentally different subset of society, and T. C. Christensen was all too happy to fall into that demographic. "A Harley is a Harley," he explains. "They're basically an old man's motorcycle. They're big sluggers, not race-around kind of bikes."

Drawn to the sportiness of British motorcycles, Christensen rode a BSA, which he thought was one of the fastest bikes in town. Tavern racing, as he calls it, created an environment similar to the one depicted in the film *American Graffiti,* and the spoils of victory were usually beers or bucks. By wrenching at a BSA garage and racing in his spare time, most of Christensen's pursuits were dedicated to speed.

In the early fall of 1962, he laid eyes on what he would later call the *Blue Behemoth,* a Norton 650 that would change his life. "It was a great

Opposite: Christensen launches his *Hogslayer* at Edgewater Dragway in Cleves, Ohio.

Spectacular burnouts
were an integral part
of the *Hogslayer*'s
mystique.

big Atlas kind of motorcycle—big, bulbous fenders—all painted blue. It ran real weird, like the primary pilot adjuster was plugged up. When revved, it went, 'riiing-pah-pah-pah-BAANG.'" Christensen, put off by its strange sights and sounds, wrote it off as a piece of junk.

Complementing the peculiarity of the bike was its owner, a one-armed man who was paying someone to race his bike. In spite of its strange idle, the *Blue Behemoth* turned out to be shockingly fast, and during a street race, it blew past Christensen's buddy's BSA. Christensen was smitten with the bike's brutish speed—he had to have one.

Just a few weeks after beating Christensen's friend, that very Norton 650 would enter Christensen's life through a strange twist of fate. While the bike's owner was riding away from a party, he accelerated to about 90 miles per hour before he was cut off by a car. The impact killed him, and Christensen ended up buying the wreckage, hoping he could build a dedicated race bike. Incorporating a Triumph rigid frame, he implanted the Norton engine, adding a full fairing and a large rear wheel. "I was blazin' the streets of Kenosha with that bike," he reminisces. "It was trick; the fastest thing on wheels by far."

His ride was so quick that he took it to the Union Road drag strip and the Great Lakes Dragaway, where he competed in his first legitimate races and won in the top gas category—with what was essentially a street bike. Lighting up the streets of Kenosha was entertaining, but Christensen quickly became addicted to legal racing, moving to nitro fuel in 1963. When his job at the American Motors factory came to an abrupt end in the late 1960s, he dedicated himself fully to racing, attending his first national drag meet in Bowling Green, Kentucky, in 1969. The event would be formative on several levels; not only would Christenson annihilate the competition and set several records, he would also see his first double-engined motorcycle, a Triumph ridden by the legendary Borris Murray from California. The bike had only one gear, and its spectacular burnouts and cannon-like exhaust notes left a deep impression on Christensen.

By 1970, he and his team built their first double-engine *Hogslayer*, so named to mock the Harley riding competition. Builder and tuner John Gregory masterminded the bike's mechanicals, and a team of machiners—well versed in fabrication from their previous jobs at the AMC factory—executed what would become the first of three *Hogslayer*s.

Because carburetors could not deliver enough fuel to the engines to make them competitive, *Hogslayer I* became one of the first drag bikes to incorporate fuel injection. The injection unit was originally intended for four-cylinder Offenhauser race car engines, and its precision was well suited for the notoriously finicky nitro-methane, which burned piston rings if the air/fuel mixture was too lean and blew up the engine if it was too rich.

The linked engines were configured so a cylinder from each would fire simultaneously, essentially causing the two powerplants to beat as one. The front motor was timed to fire a microsecond ahead of the rear, effectively removing the chain snatch and resulting in a smooth transfer of power to the meager, 4-inch-wide rear wheels. Because the bike only had one tall gear, revs had to stay high from launch, and the narrow rear tires could easily smoke their way through the entire quarter-mile. Rider skill was especially crucial with the first *Hogslayer*, as there was no room for clutch slip while the throttle was feathered in order to limit excessive wheelspin—all done without bogging down the motor. Wheel stands came easily at 70 miles per hour, creating an exciting ride for Christensen while he won races and gradually expanded his fan base.

In 1970, *Hogslayer* became the first bike to exceed 180 miles per hour in the quarter-mile, and when rivals fought back by increasing displacement, Christensen's crew countered with innovations that were simple and inventive. Taking a cue from Top Fuel drag cars, in 1972, the second iteration of the *Hogslayer* managed the twin-engine's tire-spinning torque with a makeshift slipper clutch, using bronze-sintered brakes from an earthmover. A thicker, 6-inch rear tire hooked up more effectively, and a two-speed transmission plucked from a junked AMC Rambler—its guts

The *Hogslayer* met many worthy opponents over the years, including this multiengined Harley-Davidson at Gulfport Dragway.

removed and a new case fabricated especially for the bike—enabled power to be laid down more efficiently throughout the length of the quarter-mile.

In 1972, at the World Finals in Ontario, California, the *Hogslayer* set the Top Fuel record with an elapsed time of 8.52 seconds. As it continued to dominate at the drag strip, mechanical improvements kept it on top: a thicker rear wheel accommodated 8-inch M & H slicks and the air-cooled 750-cc engines—now bored out to 880 cc—were fed by four 1⅝-inch Hilborn fuel injectors, while the engines' magneto ignition became replaced with a modern electronic system. The third iteration of the bike managed to pull the quarter-mile in the mid-7 seconds.

The bike's innovative construction was executed at Sunset Motors, Gregory's shop, which was eventually sold to Christensen. While Christensen praises his team for providing the know-how to build a bike that consistently beat Harleys at the strip, he also credits Norton for manufacturing engine components robust enough to endure the tortures of drag racing. "The more you ran it, the faster it went," he says. "I used to run the *Hogslayer* half a season, then check the compression; if the compression was up, we'd keep running it." Most teams rebuilt their engines far more frequently.

The *Hogslayer* lived up to its name so effectively, in fact, that the Harley-Davidson R&D team motivated its technicians by posting a sign in their workshop that read, "Get the Hogslayer."

Christensen's drag strip heroics were not without their mishaps, the most dramatic of which included a severe wobble in Columbus, Ohio. During a warm-up run, the steering stops snapped off and forced him to bail off the bike, sliding across the tarmac and registering a speed of 150 miles per hour, his bike careening 10 feet behind him just a half mile per hour slower. He eventually came to a stop in the fetal position, his leathers smoking from the accumulated heat of friction, and Christensen says with pride that he "went through the clocks without a bike faster than some of these guys were going on wheels." Getting away with relatively minor injuries reinforced a

While Christensen's original *Hogslayer* is now housed at the British National Motorcycle Museum, his latest iteration— the *Hogslayer III*— keeps him company in Kenosha.

recurring sensation for Christensen: that completing a race was essentially the equivalent of somebody handing his life back to him.

After nearly a decade of dominating the drag strip without factory support, the *Hogslayer* bowed out of competition in 1977, the same year that Norton went out of business. The bike's design, which was revolutionary at the time, made its place in history by bridging the sport's embryonic beginnings with what would become a 250-mile-per-hour playground of deeply funded professional teams. Terry Vance, drag racer and co-founder of performance exhaust manufacturer Vance & Hines, described Christensen as "part gunslinger, part rock star, ready to set the world on fire."

These days, Harley-Davidsons may fill the lion's share of garages in Kenosha, but T. C. Christensen's heart will always be with Norton. Christensen was inducted into the Motorcycle Hall of Fame in 2005, and the final iteration of the *Hogslayer* is now on display at the British National Motorcycle Museum. Christensen, who considers himself partially retired but still operates Sunset Motors in his hometown of Kenosha, Wisconsin, is currently bringing to life a triple-engined Norton, which he has also christened a *Hogslayer*. He affectionately refers to the bike as a "dinosaur," a term of endearment coming from a person who describes himself as a twentieth-century man stuck in the twenty-first century. His shop evokes the spirit of a time when ingenuity, hard work, and a little bit of luck had a fighting chance against a corporate giant. The patina of old machining tools and ancient parts surround the triple-engine Norton, lending a rich aura of history to the workshop that created once-mighty drag strip warriors.

T. C. Christensen on the triple-engined *Hogslayer III* in his Kenosha, Wisconsin, workshop.

A handwritten note in T. C.'s workshop says it all.

ROLLIE FREE'S
JOHN EDGAR LIGHTNING

The Bathing Suit Bike

Sometimes fame comes accidentally and sometimes it comes by surprise, but in the case of the *John Edgar Lightning*, it came entirely by design.

John Edgar, a wealthy motorcycle and car enthusiast, dreamed of owning the fastest motorcycle in America and having the time slip to prove it. Rollie Free, a cocksure racer with a lingering grudge against Harley-Davidson, hungered for speed at any cost, as long as it wasn't on a hog. Between Edgar's ambition and Free's gritty resolve, the two would, in the course of a few months, will into existence one of the most memorable motorcycles in history.

The *John Edgar Lightning* story begins over dinner. Philip Vincent, owner of the Vincent HRD motorcycle company, was in California on a sales trip when he met Edgar, who mentioned his desire to own a bike that could break the AMA speed record, which had been set at 136.183 miles per hour by Joe Petrali on a streamlined Harley-Davidson. The enterprising Vincent responded by insisting that his new Black Shadow model, with a few modifications, would be the perfect bike to break the record.

Opposite: Perhaps one of the most memorable motorcycle images of all time: Rollie Free aboard the *John Edgar Lightning* during his historic run on September 13, 1948. *Harris Vincent Gallery*

Above: Rollie Free preparing for his run. *Herb Harris*

Rollie Free pours fuel into the gas tank of the *John Edgar Lightning* in preparation for a run at Bonneville. *Herb Harris*

"If ridden by a competent rider," Vincent suggested, "the motorcycle should reach 150 mph." Stock Black Shadows, after all, could hit 125 miles per hour, and he figured that with a few modifications, there was no reason he and Edgar couldn't join forces and break Petrali's record.

In April 1948, Vincent, eager to establish his brand in the United States, finalized the agreement and cabled chief engineer Phil Irving to specially modify and ship a Black Shadow for the express purpose of beating the record. Irving had a particular gift for producing horsepower, and he determined that in order to ensure that the record was broken, the bike would need straight pipes, racing cams, larger carburetors, polished rods and flywheels, and chassis support modifications. The work would cost an extra £50, and Irving pulled the ninth Series "B" Black Shadow from the assembly line (serial number 900) to begin the transformation.

Because the engine was to run on alcohol-based fuel, the compression ratio was raised to 12.5:1. Future racing legend John Surtees was a mechanic's apprentice at the time, and he helped grind the cams—which would be referred to as Mk IIs—by hand. The standard 1⅛-inch carburetors were widened to 32 millimeters, and because of the time constraint (the Bonneville speed runs were in September), the carbs were side-mounted to the engine, without manifolds, using a special fitting between the float and mixing chambers—a setup that had been employed in the prewar

The *John Edgar Lightning* passes by a Bonneville crowd; its lack of seat made for an awkward riding posture until Rollie Free extended his legs onto the rear fender. *Herb Harris*

Series "A" Rapide model. Cylinder heads were modified, ported, and polished, and a new, more robust clutch was fitted. The bike also featured a rear hydraulic damper, one of several innovations that would later become incorporated into production Vincents.

Factory rider George Brown tested the bike at Gransden air base and reported approaching 143 miles per hour before running out of tarmac, a speed deemed sufficient for the record attempt. Then, the bike was crated up and shipped to the States, where it arrived a mere three weeks before the Bonneville runs. Rollie Free took the opportunity as a challenge—particularly because the invitation was qualified with Philip Vincent's proclamation that his Lightning could break the record if ridden by a competent rider. With precious few days remaining to make adjustments to the bike, Free stripped it of unnecessary parts and fit it to his body. A fanatic about aerodynamics and the reduction of wind resistance, Rollie modified the bike's controls to make it more slippery, sawed down the handlebars so he could tuck his arms in, and streamlined the front end by taping up the girder-style forks. Having practiced his unique style of lying on his belly and extending his legs on an Indian at Daytona, he removed the Vincent's large seat so he could lie flat on its tank. Concerned that the bike's rear aluminum fender would collapse under his weight, Free installed a sturdier steel mudguard. For extra stability, his friend Ted Piazzano constructed a wooden block to use as a foot support. Mobil Oil's sponsorship led to the incorporation of an oil can at the tail (though its promotional possibilities were somewhat muted by a thin layer of paint). The passenger footpegs were scraped down (again, to create a narrower profile) and would be used to prop Free's feet until he reached the ultimate, horizontal posture. Free would fine-tune the bike's ergonomics (and

Rollie Free cuts a distinctive silhouette across the salt flats on the *John Edgar Lightning*. Herb Harris

subsequently, his aerodynamics) by repeatedly lying out and having friends evaluate the size of the frontal surface area created by his posture.

Rollie Free worked as a gas station attendant, but his racing experience was broad. Not only was he known as the fastest street racer in Los Angeles, he had also board tracked, competed in the Indy 500, and accumulated quite a bit of hands-on mechanical experience. Wishing to improve upon the already heavily modified bike, he used 10-weight motor oil to reduce internal engine resistance and minimized rolling resistance by coating the wheel bearings with Vaseline. He reduced the wheel weight by shaving the insides and outsides of the rims, and applied wood filler to protect the inner tube from the newly exposed spokes, thereby ensuring perfectly trued wheels. By September 13, 1948, the bike was as ready as it could be, and it was finally time for it to cut through the cool morning air of Utah's salt flats.

With the help of Edgar, Rollie's army buddy Mel Held, and his mechanic Bill Demott, Free

Rollie Free, on the left, seen wearing his swimming trunks and leather jacket. *Herb Harris*

made final adjustments, push-started his bike, and set off toward the horizon. Using a line of oil in the salt as a guide, Free kept his eyes glued to the dark streak (which lined up directly behind the gear indicator), accelerated, and tucked in as he shifted the bike's tall gears and roared across the landscape. First gear took him to 100 miles per hour, and the engine, which redlined at 6,400 rpm, wound up and dropped through each of the four gears, at which point he extended his legs back and hoped for the record. He hit an average speed of 148.6 miles per hour and beat Harley-Davidson's 11-year-old record, but Free wasn't satisfied. Having come so close to the 150-mile-per-hour mark, he took an inventory of what could be improved upon in order to pass the mythical ton-and-a-half mark. The leathers he wore, which were loose and baggy (as was typical for the period), had flapped so vigorously at speed that their stitching had come undone, causing them to pull air and billow. Free figured that another run with slightly less aerodynamic drag might enable him to surpass 150 miles per hour, so he fearlessly ditched his leathers, helmet, and boots, and wore only his bathing suit, a blue bathing cap, and a friend's size 11 tennis shoes (which were several sizes too large, a fact he would later remark probably cost him a half mile per hour). With caution thrown to the desert wind, Free sped across the salt once more—streamlined and sleek—and achieved an average top speed of 150.313 miles per hour—a new American record and a memorable milestone that would make himself, John Edgar, and Vincent motorcycles household names. After the run, Rollie attributed his bathing suit idea to another racer. "I stole the swimming trunks idea from Ed Kretz, who used to do the same on Southern California dry lakes," he explained. "Incidentally, Ed looks much nicer in a swimsuit than I do."

The *John Edgar Lightning*'s success at Bonneville brought the British manufacturer immense notoriety and thrust John Edgar and Rollie Free into the limelight. Because of the buzz created by its speed, the specially prepared Black Shadow would essentially become a prototype for the future Black Lightning model. Print ads accompanied with photos of Rollie Free would later proclaim the Black Lightning "The World's Fastest Standard Motorcycle," emphasizing that "This Is a Fact, Not a Slogan." Sales of Vincents spiked from the publicity of Rollie Free's Bonneville record, but the event's publicity could not maintain Vincent's long-term success, and the company eventually went into receivership in 1959.

The *John Edgar Lightning*, which also came to be referred to as the "Bathing Suit Bike," would experience a series of ownership controversies following Rollie Free's historic run. Edgar had the bike de-tuned so it could run on pump gas and enjoyed riding it on the streets of Los Angeles with straight pipes, no headlight, no seat, and the full delight that he was on the fastest motorcycle in America. He enthusiastically loaned it to racers including Marty Dickerson and Don Vesco, and after tiring of riding the bike, he left it with an acquaintance, Allen Tompkins. Tompkins eventually left for Japan on business, and the bike was sold to a succession of air force personnel, none of whom could make it run. The last of these put a bike he owned—a Honda—up for sale in the fall of 1964. When a college student by the name of Mike Achorn came to take a look at the Honda, he caught a glimpse of the *Lightning*'s tail in the garage. Not surprisingly, he suddenly lost interest in the Honda and inquired about the Vincent. After some discussion, they agreed on a sale price of $200. Because Achorn could not afford the entire sum, he borrowed $150 from his future wife, Margaret, and contributed $50 of his own money. Using a bill of sale, the

Free's monumental accomplishment opened the floodgates to numerous promotional opportunities, including this Mobil Oil advertisement. *Herb Harris*

The *John Edgar Lightning* is currently owned by Herb Harris, who restored it to the configuration in which it achieved a two-way average speed of 150.313 miles per hour.

bike traded hands and became the property of Mike and Margaret Achorn, who hauled the motorcycle to a Vincent specialist to get it running.

Coincidentally, the mechanic who performed the work was none other than Marty Dickerson. He examined the bike, which had lost the Mobil Pegasus logo from the tank and gained a headlight. When he inspected it and gazed down into the engine, he instantly knew what it was. "Do you know what you have here?" he asked. Achorn didn't (he had been told it was a spare bike for a record attempt), and furthermore, he had no interest in treating the bike like a sacred cow. Dickerson took his orders to bring it back to life, and the Achorns would use the bike—which was equipped with stock pistons—for weekend entertainment.

The Achorns eventually moved to Michigan, and they took the *John Edgar Lightning* with them. After owning it for some 30 years, they decided upon their retirement to put it up for sale. When Texas lawyer and collector Herb Harris caught wind of the potential sale, he called the Achorns and asked to speak to Mike. Margaret, who answered the phone, announced that she was the legal owner, since she had put up most of the money and was never paid back. She was, it turned out, pulling his leg, and after speaking with Mike on the phone, Harris negotiated with the couple, agreed on a price, and drove his truck to Michigan to pick up the bike. Harris received the *John Edgar Lightning*, its related spare parts, and a Michigan certificate of title, which he would convert to a Texas certificate of title.

Ownership, particularly of historical objects of significant sentimental and monetary value, can generate ill will. When John Edgar died, debate arose regarding ownership of the famous bike.

Going through his father's possessions, Edgar's son found the *Lightning*'s pink slip, leading him to believe that he was the rightful owner. Harris explains that when he purchased the bike, he "didn't want to become the next installment in 'He stole my bike.'" Nonetheless, possession of the motorcycle instigated Edgar Jr.'s contention. The two communicated via facsimile numerous times—in less than friendly terms—to no end. Mutual friend Bruce Meyers sent a letter co-addressed to Edgar and Harris suggesting that they were both men of their word and that there ought to be a way to resolve the dispute.

Eventually, the two privately agreed to settle the matter through Harris' purchase of Edgar's ownership claim, evidenced by the original pink slip, which effectively eliminated any doubt as to the bike's ownership. Equipped with Edgar Sr.'s copious photographs of the bike, including 12 angles shot the weekend before the record-setting run, Harris used the original racing parts and restored the *Lightning* to the configuration in which it broke the speed record.

A large tachometer enabled Rollie Free to know when to shift gears.

Of all the evidence of Free's famous run—the documentation, the widespread press exposure, and of course, the *John Edgar Lightning*—the object that has touched the most people is the photograph taken from a car driving alongside the motorcycle during its record-setting run across the salt flats. Rollie Free, stripped of his leathers, his helmet, and most importantly his fear, stretches his arms forward and his legs back, risking his life in order to outdo the record he had set minutes earlier, and creates one of the most memorable images in modern motorcycling history. It is with Free's bold gesture that a great act became a truly legendary one, transforming owner, rider, and motorcycle forever.

Left: An oil can was integrated at the tail of the bike as a nod to Mobil, one of John Edgar's sponsors.

Right: Rear hydraulic dampers were unique to the *John Edgar Lightning* and would later be incorporated into production Vincents.

5

MERT LAWWILL'S
No. 1 1969
HARLEY-DAVIDSON KR750

Final Victory for a Battle-Ax

The KR750 was a battle-ax of a bike that served Harley-Davidson extraordinarily well for 16 years of the AMA Grand National series. Winning 12 of the first 13 years of the circuit, KRs edged out lighter British motorcycles, such as Triumphs and BSAs, and met a great partner in Idaho-born Mert Lawwill, who signed to race for Harley-Davidson in 1964. The hard-working racer won his first AMA national at the Sacramento Mile in 1965 and appeared to have an instinctive mastery of the Harley-Davidson KR.

The KR750 dirt tracker distinguished itself from overhead-valve 500-cc bikes with its side-valve design, which handicapped the engine's output enough for the AMA rule book to warrant its larger displacement. The 744-cc V-twin produced only 48 horsepower, but in a field of bikes sporting essentially the same power output, success came from smart chassis tuning and rider skill. "You had to be very delicate and sensitive

Opposite: Mert Lawwill astride his No. 1 bike in 1970. *Mert Lawwill collection*

AS-48

Above: Lawwill, in the center, barreling down a straightaway. *Mert Lawwill collection*

Right: Lawwill slides his 1969 KR750. *Mert Lawwill collection*

with feel and traction to win with the KR," recalls Lawwill, who was able to coax stunning performances from his Harley. While riding skill alone was not enough to make a winner, Lawwill's ability to manipulate his bike's setup lent him a significant competitive edge.

"I think where I gained my biggest advantage," he says, "was in chassis design." Learning from Jim Belland, who constructed some of Lawwill's early frames, Lawwill distinguished himself with his clever manipulation of geometry and weight distribution. The KR750's original design featured a rigid rear suspension, and Lawwill enhanced its handling by incorporating a custom frame with dual rear shocks and a steeper steering-head angle. Through his hard work developing the KR, he maximized its maneuverability and wrung out performances that would make it one of his all-time favorite bikes.

Mert Lawwill's 1969 KR750 is presently owned by Al Bergstrom.

The Harley-Davidson KR750's powerplant produced a modest 48 horsepower but won 12 of the first 13 years of the AMA Grand National series.

During the 1969 season, Lawwill's smooth but aggressive riding and his finely tuned KR's chassis proved to be an effective combination. With four race victories (including the final Grand National race of the season, which would be the last competition for the bike), he ended the age of the KR with a championship title, while also winning the AMA's Most Popular Rider award.

The following season saw the lifting of the 500-cc limit on overhead-valve engines and Harley's implementation of its XR750 line, which started life with more than its share of teething problems. That year, the documentary *On Any Sunday* captured the afterglow of Lawwill's 1969 championship and his difficulties in dealing with the new bike's unreliability. "It was devastating," Lawwill says, "mainly because the [XR750] engine was not designed to be a racing engine. It was simply a de-stroked Sportster, which was cast iron and tended to overheat." Lawwill's calm, unblinking composure was captured in gorgeously shot, slow-motion sequences that immortalized his graceful technique. While the action sequences were poetic and visually stunning, the film also demystified the life of a professional racer by showing Lawwill forming engine parts on a bench grinder and portraying a fraction of the 70,000 miles he drove per year in order to get himself to competitions.

In the film, narrator and director Bruce Brown says, "The plate he'd ridden twelve years to win and ridden one season, he'd now have to give to somebody else." The mood depicted in the

Left: Mert Lawwill's KR750 sports Harley-Davidson's No. 1 logo, which was designed in 1970 to celebrate his AMA Grand National title. **Right:** His dominating performances gave Mert Lawwill every reason to smile during the 1969 season.

documentary is one seen often in racing, a time in which a piece of equipment and a rider enjoy a final moment of glory before the winds of change turn their hard-fought victories into history.

Following the season profiled in the film, Lawwill continued a 19-year stretch of racing that eventually boasted 161 career AMA Grand National finishes and 17 National Championship wins from TT, short-track, ½-mile, 1-mile, and road-racing events. His career was cut short in 1977, when he retired due to an inner-ear disorder that impaired his equilibrium. While he would go on to design race motorcycles, bicycle suspension systems, and a prosthesis that enables amputees to grasp handlebars, Lawwill will always represent a time in Harley-Davidson's history when the KR750 dirt tracker enjoyed one last victory against the ascending British bikes.

Mert Lawwill's 1969 KR750, now owned by Al Bergstrom, paved the way for Harley's XR series of motorcycles, the success of which has extended to contemporary racing. As a critical component of the storied manufacturer's history, Mert Lawwill enjoyed the thrill of piloting a KR series bike at the end of its heyday. His No. 1 KR750 represents the final iteration of a remarkably durable design and the resolute determination of its rider.

6

EASY RIDER'S
CAPTAIN AMERICA

A Star-Spangled American Icon

Rare is the motorcycle that becomes a cultural icon, and even rarer is one that captures the *zeitgeist* of a generation. *Captain America*, the heavily customized Harley-Davidson Panhead that made its film debut during the tumultuous summer of 1969, arguably deserves both titles.

The film *Easy Rider* was released amid a maelstrom of social upheaval created by race riots, the Vietnam War, and a burgeoning counterculture movement that challenged the perceived establishment. Following the lucrative drug deal that opens the film, Peter Fonda and Dennis Hopper acquire outlandishly tricked-out Harleys. They stash their cash in *Captain America*'s gas tank and set out for what could be considered the American dream: financial stability and ultimate freedom.

The motorcycle that would become the mechanical manifestation of the anti-establishment was sourced from an unlikely place: a police auction. Purchased for $500 along with three other bikes—a backup *Captain*

Opposite: Peter Fonda rides *Captain America* during the filming of *Easy Rider*. The Harley's 43-degree fork rake made it extremely difficult to maneuver at low speeds. *Corbis*

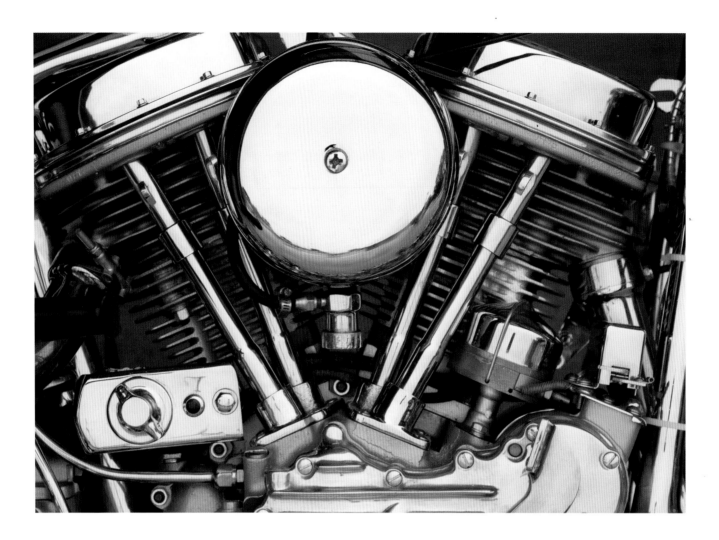

At the heart of this chopper is a chromed 1,200-cc V-twin engine.

America and two so-called "Billy" bikes—the nearly 20-year-old motorcycles were modified by Cliff Vaughs and Ben Hardy based on Fonda's vision. "I'd designed the extended and mildly raked front forks, helmet, sissy bar, and the tank," Fonda would later say, though Vaughs' chop job produced a ridiculous rake angle of 43 degrees.

From its extensively chromed rigid-wishbone frame to its exaggerated ape-hanger bars resting on two risers, *Captain America*'s lavish appearance was perfectly suited to the ambitions and excesses of Fonda's character, Wyatt. The peanut tank boasted an American flag design painted by famed pinstriper Von Dutch, and the angled fish-head exhaust pipes and sissy bar artfully complemented the upswept lines created by the bike's forks. To become acquainted with the bike's peculiar handling characteristics, Fonda spent a week prior to the film's production riding it on Los Angeles freeways. Decked out in the stars-and-stripes jacket he would wear during filming, Fonda was repeatedly pulled over by police, reinforcing the widely held stereotype of bikers as outlaws that would be depicted in the film's storyline.

The slow speeds required during the filming process took a toll on Fonda. "It was a major bitch to ride," he said. "The first day [of shooting] we went from Needles to Kingman, Arizona— that's 55 miles. It took a day to get there." Riding the bikes may have been awkward, but director Dennis Hopper and cinematographer Laszlo Kovacs transformed the experience into a visually poetic and viscerally moving ode to the American road trip. The journey of Wyatt and Billy, though filled with exploration and adventure, ultimately takes a dark turn in a scene where Billy

John Parham's motorcycle was rebuilt by Dan Haggerty, allegedly using parts from the wreckage of the original *Captain America*. It was photographed near the National Motorcycle Museum, where it is on permanent display.

An upswept sissy
bar and fishtail
exhaust pipes
complement the bike's
angled visual cues.

declares, triumphantly, "We're rich!" to which Wyatt responds, "We blew it." The phrase appears to discount Billy's equation of wealth with success, supporting the concept that freedom is more elusive than a tank full of cash and freewheeled rambling. At the end of the film, close to their destination, Wyatt and Billy are senselessly gunned down by two men in a pickup truck, and their bikes are destroyed along with their dreams.

The existence of the real *Captain America* motorcycle has been the subject of much speculation. It is widely agreed that the two Billy bikes and one of the two *Captain America* bikes were stolen just before the completion of filming, never to be recovered. The fate of the *Captain America* motorcycle that was destroyed in the final scene of the movie, however, is more convoluted. According to one source, the wreckage of the *Captain America* bike was gifted to Dan Haggerty (who handled the bike during production) as a memento from Peter Fonda. Haggerty allegedly restored the bike in his Woodland Hills, California, home, and after it didn't meet reserve at one auction, John Parham purchased it at another auction. Though he prefers not to disclose the purchase price, Parham says, "I paid a lot for it. You can buy a nice, decent house for that price." Parham asserts that a certificate of authenticity signed by Fonda and Haggerty validates the bike's roots, but Texas resident Gordon Granger also owns what he believes is the real *Captain America*, and he also possesses a certificate signed by Haggerty claiming authenticity.

Whether or not pieces of the original *Captain America* exist in either of the two motorcycles is an endlessly debatable topic, but what transcends that argument is the historical context of what the bike represents. Perhaps more than any other motorcycle, it reflects a turbulent moment in history when the future of the United States was as uncertain as the open road. Iconic, bold, and unapologetic, *Captain America* has become a visual symbol for the ideals and dreams of an era that have all but disappeared, making it perhaps one of the most recognizable and evocative motorcycles of all time.

The heavily customized Harley-Davidson Panhead boasts an unmistakable stance.

7

DICK MANN'S
BSA GOLD STAR AND MATCHLESS G50 TT

The Tools of the Trade

Dick Mann had his first two-wheeled experiences while delivering newspapers during grade school, and though his Cushman scooter lacked speed, it stirred up his competitive spirit. "Some of the greatest, wackiest bike races in the history of the world took place while we worked on our paper routes," he wrote in his 1972 autobiography. "We were young, didn't know the meaning of fear, and always refused to back down."

Not much would change as Mann grew up; he would later enjoy cow trailing his 250-cc BSA Bantam in the hills of Richmond, California, and follow his passion by ditching a well-paid job at Standard Oil to work at a BSA dealership. His duties were comprehensive; not only did he learn how to tune, repair, and weld, he also became a skilled painter and pin-striper. In 1954, he raced in the amateur class at the Bay Meadows mile. Learning the ropes of motorcycle racing was, almost literally, a trial by fire. By the end of the race, his skid shoe had disintegrated, begun smoking,

Opposite: Dick Mann resting on his BSA Gold Star dirt tracker at the Sacramento Mile in 1968. *Dave Friedman photo/Don Emde collection*

Mann was involved in every stage of the Gold Star's restoration, including painting and pinstriping.

and nearly caught on fire—but he won. Encouraged by this victory, Mann cut his teeth by traveling and competing under the tutelage of racer Al Gunter. Learning from the seasoned pro, he was instilled with an innate sense of what it took to win at the racetrack. Not only would he adopt Gunter's take-no-prisoners attitude, he would also become steeped in curious disciplines, such as how to ride with intensely painful injuries and how to manage the controlled chaos of life as an itinerant racer.

Riding on a factory-sponsored Harley-Davidson at Daytona in 1958, Mann quickly learned that competing on somebody else's bike resulted in significantly less earnings. Though factory support carried a certain level of prestige, he decided to race primarily through his own means on his own machines. After all, racing was his life, and business was as much a part of his plan as was adventure. Though he occasionally accepted sponsorship opportunities, he would rely on two personal bikes—a BSA Gold Star dirt tracker and a Matchless G50 TT bike—as workhorses that carried him through years of hard racing. The BSA, which he raced between 1958 and 1968, and the Matchless, which he competed on between 1961 and 1968, were vehicles he became intimately acquainted with while building, tuning, and rebuilding them by hand from season to season.

As Mann's career progressed, so did his reputation as a serious, dedicated, and versatile performer who competed with fierce reliability. When his left hand was injured and unable to grip, he had it taped to the handlebar so he could finish a race. In 1966, he suffered through most of the season with a broken collarbone and a pin sticking out of his shoulder. His solution? Cut his leathers to accommodate the protrusion and ride through the pain. At a race in Sacramento in 1970, he cut off his cast and rode with a broken ankle, an act captured in the documentary *On Any Sunday*. Mann was famous for saying, "If you race bikes for a living and need the dough, and your injury isn't going to kill you, I say ignore it!" With a stiff upper lip, he pressed through the pitfalls of racing, stoically finishing race after race through a love of the sport and the sheer will to succeed.

Because of his hands-on mechanical experience and inventive nature, Mann developed new ways to make his bikes work better. The BSA and the Matchless became test beds that eventually enabled him to develop adjustable footpegs, a composite one-piece seat/rear fender/number plate piece that removed easily for quick maintenance, and the first-ever air filter for dirt tracking. He was also the first to develop an adjustable wheel camber system on his Gold Star to enable the bike to handle better on left turns.

Mann's reliance on his bikes required him to configure them as efficient, trustworthy instruments. While racers often make the mistake of coaxing maximum power out of their engines at any expense, Mann tuned for consistency, trading a few extra horsepower for dependability. Adaptability was also key; because his Matchless could be set up for TT, road racing, or dirt tracking by changing wheels, footpegs, gearing, and exhaust configuration, the bike served Mann very well

Above: Dick Mann's BSA Gold Star is regularly raced at vintage events by owner Fred Mork.

Left: Mann slides his BSA at Tulare, California.
Dan Mahony

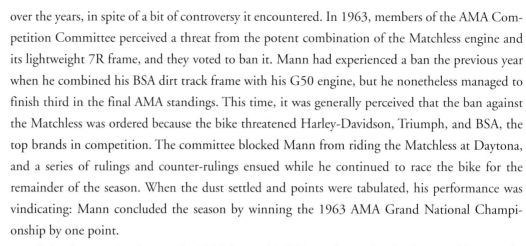

Opposite top: Mann's Matchless G50 TT is currently owned by Robert Iannucci.
Below: Mann flying his Matchless G50 in TT mode at Ascot in 1964. *Dan Mahony*

A rider's view of the Matchless G50 TT.

over the years, in spite of a bit of controversy it encountered. In 1963, members of the AMA Competition Committee perceived a threat from the potent combination of the Matchless engine and its lightweight 7R frame, and they voted to ban it. Mann had experienced a ban the previous year when he combined his BSA dirt track frame with his G50 engine, but he nonetheless managed to finish third in the final AMA standings. This time, it was generally perceived that the ban against the Matchless was ordered because the bike threatened Harley-Davidson, Triumph, and BSA, the top brands in competition. The committee blocked Mann from riding the Matchless at Daytona, and a series of rulings and counter-rulings ensued while he continued to race the bike for the remainder of the season. When the dust settled and points were tabulated, his performance was vindicating: Mann concluded the season by winning the 1963 AMA Grand National Championship by one point.

Going into semi-retirement in 1966, he put his BSA on the market for $500 and his Matchless for $1,500 and moved to Hawaii to work as a motorcycle salesman. Retail work, it turned out, did not complement Mann's quiet personality, and he quickly found life on the island paradise was anything but. He moved back from Hawaii, lifted his bikes off the market, and returned to full-time racing while consulting and designing frames for OSSA and Yankee motorcycles. By 1969, Mann—at the age of 35—was considered too old to race by BSA brass and was dropped from the team. Picked up by Honda, he rode at Daytona (a race he had completed as a runner-up three times before but had never won) and took the top spot. In 1971, he returned to BSA at the age of 37 and earned his second AMA Grand National Championship, becoming the oldest rider to win the title. That year, Mann also became the first rider to win the AMA Grand Slam, which included mile, half-mile, short-track, TT, and road-racing events. He also was awarded Man of the Year honors by *Cycle* and *Motorcycle Weekly* magazines and was christened the AMA's Most Popular Rider. Between 1957 and 1973, he finished in the Grand National top 10 for all but one year. He represented the United States in the Transatlantic Match Race and the International Six Days Trial, where he won a bronze medal, and finally retired from the Grand National circuit in 1974.

Though Dick Mann's career saw him race for a number of nameplates, he earned the unofficial title of the "ultimate privateer," primarily because of his exploits with two personal bikes. When asked if his motorcycles were like companions during the years he campaigned them, he responds, "That sounds very romantic, but they were actually tools—I was like a woodsman with the same ax for thirty years." Indeed, through countless engines, clutches, and transmissions, Dick Mann took good care of his bikes, and in turn they took good care of him. The BSA dirt

tracker, which Mann restored and owned for over 20 years after retiring it, was eventually sold to Fred Mork, who keeps it exercised by racing it at vintage events. The Matchless, which endured controversy with the AMA but emerged victorious in the 1963 Grand National Championship, is now owned by Robert Iannucci. Mann, who lives in Nevada, still enjoys off-road motorcycling and restoring British single-cylinder bikes.

His self-sustained career with the BSA Gold Star and Matchless G50 TT proved that before the era of corporate race teams, a talented privateer could rise to greatness. Dick Mann, in his typically humble and understated manner, has often insisted that he was not a natural-born racer. However, his motivation, hard work, and mechanical innovations turned him and his bikes into winners.

8

FREDDIE SPENCER'S

1985 DOUBLE CHAMPIONSHIP HONDA GP BIKES

Living the Impossible Dream

History is littered with fast race bikes and talented racers, but the perfect storm of mechanical excellence and superlative human skill is far less common. In 1980, an 18-year-old phenom named Freddie Spencer stunned the world by beating former Grand Prix World Champions Kenny Roberts and Barry Sheene at Britain's Transatlantic Match Races on an Erv Kanemoto–tuned Yamaha TZ750. Following his earlier Superbike victories, Spencer had caught the attention of Honda Racing Corporation founder Shoichiro Irimajiri, who craved a 500-cc World Championship. Honda took a chance on Spencer, who met their expectations by becoming the youngest World Grand Prix Champion in 1983 at the age of 21. By 1984, Honda's newly redesigned 500-cc bike revealed the extent of the company's desire to capture another world championship. The two-stroke NSR-500 (NV0A), rigorously tested with Spencer's feedback, featured engineering advances intended to ensure Honda's dominance in

Opposite: Freddie Spencer enjoys victory at the 1985 500-cc Swedish Grand Prix. *Stan Perec*

Above: Spencer hugs the apex at the Swedish Grand Prix. *Stan Perec*

Right: Following the exploding carbon wheel debacle of 1984, Spencer was relieved that his 1985 bikes were reliable.

Grand Prix racing. The quantum leaps were so extreme, in fact, that that bike ended up forcing Spencer to fight not only his competitors but also the bike itself.

For instance, the fuel tank was positioned below the engine in the interest of mass centralization, but the unorthodox placement caused the exhaust—which ran past the false gas tank above the motor—to melt the bike's body, creating dangerous fumes and scorching Spencer's chest in its first race, the Daytona 200. Carbon-fiber wheels, never before incorporated into a GP bike, seemed like an ideal way to reduce unsprung weight—until one exploded during qualifying after Spencer achieved pole position at the first Grand Prix in South Africa, breaking both of his feet and forcing him to miss several races. The position of the fuel tank, in spite of baffles that were fitted later, affected fuel stability during cornering at high-altitude tracks, resulting in the occasional interruption of power during high g-force turns.

The 500-cc bike was built entirely by hand, as evidenced by the irregular weld seams on the fuel tank.

Still, radical technological advances are a mandatory component of Grand Prix racing, and Spencer coped remarkably well with the 1984 bike's shortcomings. He ended the season with five victories and finished in fourth place overall. Spencer reflects that "being at the front certainly has its downside; it taught us some hard lessons." But those failures led to Honda's incorporation of a lower center of gravity and the implementation of a higher rear ride height and greater rake and trail, which aided handling.

During downtime at Assen in June 1984, after a spark plug cap failure knocked him out of the race, Spencer and his crew began discussing the upcoming 1985 season. The conversation inevitably evolved into a discussion about attempting the seemingly impossible: what if Freddie Spencer simultaneously competed in the 250-cc and 500-cc competitions? The concept was, in

Though similar to the 250-cc bike at first glance, the 500-cc provided a completely different riding experience.

fact, quite out of reach, since Honda did not have a 250-cc GP bike. Regardless of that glaring limitation, Honda was a company of great ambitions and Spencer was a racer with similarly lofty desires. Within three months, Satoru Horiike designed and built a two-cylinder V-twin 250-cc bike that Spencer would pilot—as well as a 500-cc bike with a newly designed V4 engine—in hopes of capturing both 1985 championships.

Spencer's consistency in providing telemetry to 250-cc chief mechanic Stewart Shenton and crew chief Erv Kanemoto aided the development process, and because working on both bikes meant back-to-back meetings with both crews, he multitasked while keeping his eye on what Honda considered the main prize: the 500-cc competition. "I had to compartmentalize the two," he recalls, "remember what each was doing, and make sure we were always moving in the right direction." Not only did the back-to-back practice sessions prepare him mentally for switching between the two (some races featured the lower-displacement event first, others were vice versa), Spencer also underwent physical training that included weights, bicycling, basketball, and tennis. Though his body weight had dropped down to 146 pounds, he was still a bit heavy compared to the top 250-cc competitors, who hovered in the 120–130-pound range. Conversely though, he was lighter than most 500-cc racers, which presented its own challenges in the 500-cc class since a certain amount of heft makes it easier to control the heavier, more powerful bikes.

Though he was in outstanding shape, the dynamics of both bikes necessitated two different mental game plans. The 250-cc relied more on corner speed and momentum, requiring precise rider input to yield a competitive performance. The 500-cc, on the other hand, spent less time on the side of its tires and was far less forgiving at its limit—which Spencer pushed with his innovative technique of scrubbing the front tires and sliding out the back. The larger bike's intrinsically narrow powerband had been improved by the 1985 season, but it still left little margin for error. Spencer describes his tactics: "I'd give myself one lap to get up to speed on the 250 or 500. That forced me into my entry point, direction change, and lean angle to get the bike in the right position for maximum acceleration."

Spencer at full lean in the 250-cc French Grand Prix, his last 250-cc race of the 1985 season, which he won. *Stan Perec*

As Spencer dove into the 1985 season, the bikes experienced ongoing modifications. He went through 500 Michelin tires during winter preseason in the hope of finding the ideal setup. But because radial technology was still new, severe chatter problems forced him to start the season with rear radials and front bias-belted tires. The arrangement required chassis compensations until front radials were incorporated a few races later. The series opener at the South African Grand Prix saw him finish first in the 250-cc class and second in the 500-cc, and while he won the next 500-cc race at the Spanish Grand Prix and appeared to have the 250-cc event wrapped up, his exhaust pipe split, thwarting his efforts and forcing him to finish in ninth place.

Race logistics often meant a mad scramble in order to start the second event, and at the 500-cc Grand Prix at Mugello, Italy, Spencer fought and won a difficult battle with Eddie Lawson and Christian Sarron. After appearing on the podium and rehydrating by drinking as much water as possible, he returned to the staging area to find that the 250-cc competitors were already gone—with the exception of multiple 250-cc champion Tony Mang, who thought it proper to wait for Spencer.

Single-mindedly focused on the duality of his unique task, Spencer pressed on, and his comfortable points lead in the 250-cc class allowed him to drop out of the last two races to more effectively

The 250-cc bike's compact proportions made it more maneuverable than the larger 500-cc bike.

Freddie Spencer's
1985 double
championship bikes in
a rare moment
together. *American
Honda Motor Co., Inc.*

focus his efforts on 500-cc. By season's end, Spencer achieved 15 pole positions, set nine new track records, and won 14 races. In addition to his double Grand Prix championship, earlier in March 1985, Spencer won all three divisions at Daytona Speed Week—250-cc Expert, 500-cc Formula 1, and Superbike.

Such landmark achievements gave Freddie Spencer the appearance of invincibility, but the physical demands of testing and racing during his watershed year subjected his body to irreversible harm. Flying back and forth to the United States for medical treatment, Spencer battled nerve, ligament, and tendon damage, and in spite of surgeries on his wrist, hand, and neck, he was unable to continue racing. He retired in 1988 and attempted several comebacks. He won his final competition, an AMA National at Laguna Seca in 1995, by a wide margin, with his lead measuring 23 seconds at one point during the race. Following his retirement, Spencer founded the Freddie

Spencer Performance Riding School, where he passes on the skills he developed during his almost 30 years of international motorcycle racing.

The NSR-250 bike raced by Spencer during his historic double championship sits in the office of his Las Vegas residence, and the NSR-500 (NV0B) has been restored to race condition and is a part of Honda's Collection Hall exhibit at Motegi, Japan. Spencer occasionally rides demonstration laps with the 500-cc bike at events such as the Goodwood Festival of Speed.

While he paid a steep physical price for his pursuit of two championships during the same year, Spencer's accomplishments have yet to be attempted, let alone matched, by any other racer. Groundbreaking and brazenly ambitious, Freddie Spencer's 1985 double-championship season stands as a testimony to the extraordinary limits of one man's physical and mental abilities, and his unrelenting drive to surpass conventional definitions of success.

9

CRAIG VETTER'S
MYSTERY SHIP

The Childhood Fantasy Bike

"**M**any of the choices we make as adults," explains motorcycle designer Craig Vetter, "are rooted in our childhood." Consider the orange, yellow, and black of the Triumph Hurricane he designed in the late 1960s, for instance, and you might recognize the Lionel train paint scheme that, in Vetter's words, made his heart go "pitter patter" when he was a boy.

Vetter always had a strong desire to design his dream motorcycle, a project that would start manifesting itself in the early 1970s. Since the age of 10, he had an affinity to the enigmatic moniker of *Mystery Ship*, which refers to a sleek 1929 Beechcraft aircraft. The futuristic vision of the plane was an intrinsic part of Vetter's design DNA, and it would eventually inspire him to draft his definitive bike.

It took, however, a sequence of life experiences for the puzzle of Vetter's *Mystery Ship* to assemble itself. The success of his Windjammer fairings,

Opposite: The *Mystery Ship*'s colors were also incorporated in Vetter's Triumph Hurricane.
Above: Craig Vetter's quick sketch from 1977 depicts the basic silhouette of the *Mystery Ship. Craig Vetter collection*

The evolution of the *Mystery Ship*. Craig Vetter collection

produced since 1971, enabled him to explore road racing. In 1975, he took his Yamaha YZ250-powered motorcycle to Daytona and finished an impressive fifth in the amateur category. Vetter, who was campaigning a Rickman-framed bike in the anything-goes Café class in 1975, became the Midwest champion with a 1,100-cc-engined motorcycle that featured exotic aluminum wheels and plasma-covered brake rotors. A third-place finish at Daytona in 1976 furthered his interest in incorporating race technology into street bikes. However, he eventually came to the realization that "there was not a single thing I could translate from the racetrack to the street." It seemed that his *Mystery Ship* mockup on the stiff-framed Rickman was never going to become the smooth-riding luxo-cruiser he yearned to produce, and his dream lingered in limbo.

Vetter's path toward the *Mystery Ship* became even more circuitous when he suffered a severe crash at Road Atlanta in 1976. Immediately following the accident, a witness approached his mangled body and asked if he was alive; Vetter would remain in traction for three months, and his fiancée, Carol, finally drew the line by barring him from road racing. When he visited California the following year, Vetter met Cook Neilson and Phil Schilling, who told him about Superbike, an exciting new class of racing that involved modified versions of production motorcycles. Intrigued by their proposal but reluctant to expose himself to further physical risk, Vetter asked who they would pick for a dream team. They suggested tuner/builder Pierre des Roches and racer Reg Pridmore. Keith Code offered to drive the truck if he could also race, and Vetter devised a plan: he would write a $10,000 check and sponsor the first Superbike race at Laguna Seca. He went on to create the Vetter Superbike team, which would develop his *Mystery Ship* from race-proven components.

He sponsored the team under the condition that he retain the bike at the end of the season, and des Roches proceeded to modify a Kawasaki KZ1000 for racing. The KZ's notoriously flexible chassis was reinforced by bracing the frame and swingarm. Stability was improved by moving the steering head back, which also shortened the wheelbase and effectively shifted the bike's center of gravity forward. The 1,015-cc dual-overhead-cam inline-four received Yoshimura cams and pistons, a modified carburetor, a hand-formed four-into-one Bassani exhaust, a tail-mounted Lockhart oil cooler, and various other improvements that boosted horsepower to 140.

Team Vetter's No. 163 Kawasaki was so well developed, tuned, and ridden that it won the 1978 Superbike championship, leaving Vetter with the ideal benchmark for his *Mystery Ship* project. Following the victory, he promptly took the No. 163 bike to Sandy Kosman, who he considered to be the best frame builder and engineer on the West Coast. Kosman examined all the gussets, modifications, and revised geometry of des Roches' work and produced 10 exact replicas of the frame. Vetter developed radical bodywork by assembling mockups using wood mandrel that would eventually be covered with clay from which fiberglass molds would be shaped. Throughout the development process, Vetter often sat on the mockup at his San Luis Obispo workshop, experimenting with different body positions to simulate riding postures.

The first *Mystery Ship* was donated to the AMA Hall of Fame Museum in Pickerington, Ohio.

Mystery Ship No. 6, owned by Dillard Coleman, was turbocharged and painted red. *Craig Vetter collection*

The No. 9 *Mystery Ship* was turbocharged and is now a part of the Barber Vintage Motorsports Museum in Birmingham, Alabama. *Craig Vetter collection*

As the *Mystery Ship* finally came to life, Vetter's bodywork merged with the race-proven mechanicals, producing a bike that blended the Rickman-framed version's touring intentions with a more sporting edge. The angular bodywork reflected the iconic spirit of Vetter's childhood inspirations. The panels were easily removed via four bolts, and an integrated number plate just below the seat was intended to display the production number of the bike (which Vetter targeted at 200) while maintaining aerodynamic streamlining. During Vetter's time at Daytona, he observed that white was the most visible color, and by layering silver with white, he created a paint scheme reminiscent of military transport vehicles. The addition of silver, yellow, and red stripes also evoked the graphics of his Triumph Hurricane. As the design became refined, stylized slats were eliminated, and the overall look became that of flush, sharp-edged lines aimed optimistically upward.

According to Vetter, the *Mystery Ship* rode like a light streetbike, though its 495-pound dry weight also lent it a substantial feeling as it rolled down the road. The design direction was definitively American—big and bold—and *Cycle* magazine's October 1980 issue pitted the *Mystery Ship* against the characteristically Italian Bimota KB1 in its "Gold Dust Challenge" cover story. In contrast to the finely detailed, unrelentingly performance-oriented Bimota, the *Mystery Ship* was considered more comfortable and practical—in spite of its outrageous $10,000 price tag and unusual styling. "On the one hand, the *M-Ship* is a Vetter art form;" mused the writer, "on the other hand, beneath the fiberglass the hardware suggests the capability to go so fast in a nonchalant way as to place the rolling sculpture in real jeopardy. That suggestion of super-performance, strengthened by the *M-Ship*'s modified chassis, magnesium wheels, lay-down shocks and all other assorted go-fast technoware, makes you wonder exactly what Craig Vetter had in mind."

What was on Vetter's mind would change dramatically after a gust of wind rammed him and his ultralight into the ground on October 10, 1980. The moment Vetter saw his legs pointing the wrong way, he realized his life would change yet again. "I knew that would be the end of the *Mystery Ship*," he would later say, and being confined to a wheelchair galvanized him to design and build the type of human-powered vehicle that he, as a designer, would want to use. His creation turned out to be an aesthetic and functional success that enabled Jim Knaub to win the Boston Marathon in 1982.

The *Mystery Ship* had a final production run of only 10, making each example highly sought after. The first was Vetter's personal bike and was donated to the AMA Hall of Fame Museum in Pickerington, Ohio; the location of No. 2, which was painted black and known as *Darth Vetter*, is unknown; No. 3 was given away at a Vetter rally and eventually bought by Malcolm Forbes (as was No. 7.); No. 4 was used in *Cycle* magazine's "Gold Dust Challenge" and shipped to Germany for testing in *Motorrad* magazine; No. 5 was bought by Norman Jones of Kansas City and sold at auction in 2004; No. 6, owned by Dillard Coleman, was painted red and fitted with a turbocharger; No. 8 is part of the Barber Vintage Motorsports Museum collection in Birmingham, Alabama, as is No. 9, which was painted red, white, and blue, and turbocharged; No. 10 was shipped to an unknown owner in Canada.

Vetter, though proud of his achievements with the *Mystery Ship*, asserts that his fuel-economy contests are his most important accomplishments outside of raising his family. Dedicated to the pursuit of environmental responsibility, Vetter has refocused his efforts toward motorcycle design that is, above all, efficient and functional. Does he still have a soft spot for fast, radically designed motorcycles based on inspirations from his youth? "I'm not the man I was when I was 38 years old," he responds, suggesting that the *Mystery Ship* reflects the priorities, goals, and fascinations of a different time. Dreams can change, but they don't necessarily lose their intensity.

Team Vetter's 1978 Superbike-winning No. 178 bike added credibility to the *Mystery Ship*'s marketing efforts. *Craig Vetter collection*

10

CAL RAYBORN'S

No. 3 HARLEY-DAVIDSON XR750

A Transatlantic Sensation

Like many successful racers, Calvin Rayborn II made his acquaintance with speed at a young age. Taking a part-time job as a motorcycle messenger during his adolescence, he discovered the direct correlation between the expedience of his delivery and how much he was paid; before long, he dedicated himself to honing the skills that would fatten his wallet.

At its essence, racing has many similarities to the motorcycle messenger business, and during his late teens, Rayborn carried his experience to the track alongside friend and future land-speed record-breaker Don Vesco. Tackling the amateur circuit, Rayborn quickly learned that road racing was his forte, and by 1965, he turned pro. In spite of substantial setbacks, including the broken back he suffered during his first season, Rayborn continued a steady ascension. By 1966, he won his first AMA national event.

Opposite: Cal Rayborn rides his iron-barrel Harley-Davidson XR750 at the Mallory Park portion of 1972's Transatlantic Match Races. *Mick Woollett*

Rayborn's exceptional skill was creating buzz, and his performances caught the attention of Dick O'Brien, Harley's racing director, who knew greatness when he saw it. So deft were Rayborn's racing instincts, in fact, that O'Brien would later say that he considered Rayborn one of the best road racers he had ever seen.

Rayborn's rapidly accelerating career was distinctive not only due to his winning record, but also because of the innovative techniques that placed him on the podium. Particularly adept at tight, technical turns, Rayborn shined where others went too slow and lost their edge, or simply went too fast and crashed. "Nontechnical sections don't really separate the men from the boys," explains Don Emde, who raced with Rayborn. "Tires weren't great in those days, and in the more technical areas, Cal could still keep the throttle on, even sliding a bit at times, where others might be backing off the throttle to take it at a more conservative pace."

Rayborn's performance on pavement was astounding, but he did not fare as well at flat-track dirt events, and because AMA championships were based on an accumulation of points in both types of races, he would never win a title. On the road circuit, however, he reached the peak of his prowess while racing for the Harley-Davidson factory team. In 1968 and 1969, he won back-to-back victories at the Daytona 200 on a 750 KR, and he became the first rider to lap the entire field and average over 100 miles per hour during the 1968 Daytona race.

In 1970, he took his talent to Bonneville where he ran a nitromethane-burning Harley-Davidson Sportster-based streamliner designed by Denis Manning. In spite of several high-speed crashes and the fact that he had never before piloted a streamliner, Rayborn's persistence eventually led him to break the international record with a speed of 265.492 miles per hour. Dick O'Brien, already a proponent of Rayborn, had every reason to be pleased with his record-breaking performance. However, Rayborn's racing started to suffer due to reliability issues with the XR's outdated cast-iron cylinders. Nicknamed "iron barrel," the bike's engine was based on a scaled-down Sportster powerplant and was not competitive with the lighter, quicker, and more-reliable Japanese two-strokes. For the first time in five years, Rayborn went without a national victory, though in 1971, he enjoyed his first national flat-track win at Michigan's Livonia Mile.

In spite of his domestic racing victories, Rayborn's most famous performance occurred abroad. England's Transatlantic Match Races pitted American racers against the British on their home turf, but because Harley-Davidson was concerned that the reliability of the iron-barrel

The Cal Rayborn No. 3 Harley-Davidson XR750 is now a part of the AMA Motorcycle Hall of Fame Museum.

XR750 would become an international embarrassment, they refused to back Rayborn on the out-dated bike, which was due to be replaced in a matter of months. Nonetheless, in the spring of 1972, he found assistance from *Motor Cycle Weekly* magazine and decided to borrow and race his tuner's personal XR750. Rayborn flew to the event with friend and fellow Daytona 200 winner Don Emde, who drew up maps on airline cocktail napkins to give Rayborn an idea of what the tracks looked like. Racing the No. 3 Harley, Rayborn was doubly handicapped; not only had he never seen the course in person, he was also riding a machine notorious for its tendency to over-heat—and, in some cases, blow up.

At the Match Races, skill and luck proved a potent combination for Rayborn, who turned in a staggering performance. Because he possessed the rare ability to learn a course without the benefit of many practice laps, he attacked the three courses—Brand's Hatch, Mallory Park, and Oulton Park—with zeal. Aided by Britain's cool April weather, Rayborn prevailed at the first two courses, which were smaller and more technical. However, at Oulton Park, he was enjoying a lead until the XR's engine temperature started to rise, eventually causing the bike to run on only one cylinder. Nonetheless, in the final points tabulation, he won three of the six rounds of races, making him the top-scoring American and tying him with British racer Ray Pickrell for the top finish. "People were just amazed," recalls Emde, and Rayborn's victory won over European fans and helped negate the notion that American racers were gifted solely in dirt track racing.

Back in the States, Rayborn enjoyed well-earned respect for his international success. He won two nationals and earned Harley's final AMA Grand National road race victory at Laguna Seca. Because Harley-Davidson's road racing bikes were losing ground to Japanese competitors, Rayborn

As with many bikes of the period, a pad was strapped to the tank in order to protect the riders' chests when they tucked down.

made the difficult decision to leave Harley at the end of the 1973 season. Shortly after he accepted an offer to race for Suzuki, he elected to enter a club event in New Zealand. The Suzuki he was to ride had belonged to racer Geoff Perry, who died months earlier in an airplane crash. But the connection didn't faze Rayborn, who probably viewed the opportunity to ride the two-stroke as a way to hone his skills in preparation for his new association with the Japanese manufacturer. During the event, the bike's engine suddenly seized and slammed his body against a wall, killing him instantly. He was 33.

The pinnacle of Cal Rayborn's career saw him take his No. 3 Harley-Davidson to victory in spite of the bike's fading technology. The motorcycle, which is owned by the Motorcycle Hall of Fame Museum, is on display at the gallery in Pickerington, Ohio. Sporting Harley's trademark orange-and-black livery, rounded fairing, and iconic profile, the XR750 recalls an era when heroes like Cal Rayborn seemed invincible, managing to prove their supremacy on the global stage against the most daunting of odds. Despite the will of an influential manufacturer and the inadequacies of an outdated machine, the Harley represents the victory of a man over his competitors and his triumph over seemingly insurmountable circumstances.

The U.S. Transatlantic Match Races team lines up at the Oulton Park course. Cal Rayborn is at the far left, and to the right of Rayborn is Don Emde. *Don Emde collection*

11

WAYNE RAINEY'S

1983 KAWASAKI SUPERBIKE

The Air-Cooled Underdog

Wayne Rainey's path to GP racing was gradual and his departure from it sudden, but in that brief span, his ambition carried him remarkably far. Beginning his pro career in 1979 on the dirt tracks of the AMA Grand National circuit, it would take several years (including a frustrating debut season in which he was sidelined by injuries) before Rainey entered the arena where his talents truly shined: road racing. By 1980, he had earned six top-10 AMA Grand National finishes and, recognizing that Rainey might have a bright future off the dirt, Kawasaki began supporting him at the club level. His success in the novice 250-cc class allowed Kawasaki to graduate him to Superbike racing in 1982, where he became teammates with then-reigning National Champion Eddie Lawson. Rainey was only 21 years old, and Kawasaki was positioning him to be a key figure in their future racing endeavors.

Kawasaki appeared to be on the right track. Rainey finished fifth in his debut at Daytona, third in the next three rounds, and, after battling

Opposite: Wayne Rainey at the starting grid on his No. 60 Kawasaki Superbike. *Paul Schwab*
Above: Wayne Rainey muscles his Kawasaki through a turn. *Paul Schwab*

Wayne Rainey at speed on his Kawasaki Superbike.
Paul Schwab

Honda's Steve Wise at Loudon on June 19, he won his first National. The standings at the end of his rookie Superbike season placed him third behind teammate Lawson and Honda's Mike Baldwin. Rainey's solid performance during his first season of Superbike racing proved that he might possess the skill and tenacity to someday hold the racing world in the palm of his hand.

Ready to translate his incredible momentum into a second year of Superbike racing in 1983, Rainey faced daunting competition from the well-funded Honda team, which quickly adapted to a new drop in the displacement limit (from 1,025 cc to 750 cc) by debuting its impressive water-cooled, V-4 Interceptor design. Piloted by new reigning champ Mike Baldwin, the bike was a formidable competitor, especially when compared to Rainey's GPz750 bike, which was mired in old, air-cooled technology. Teammate Eddie Lawson left Superbike that year for the GP circuit, which made the relatively inexperienced Rainey the lead rider. As the season ensued, it became painfully evident that Rainey's work was cut out for him. Honda started off threateningly, taking the first six victories of the season, but Rainey didn't back down, retaliating with a fierce six-win streak of his own. By the end of the season, he and his Kawasaki beat out the technologically superior Honda, earning him his first road racing championship.

The world of racing can deliver triumphs that are inextricably linked to loss, and Rainey's first national championship turned out to be bittersweet. Kawasaki, which had groomed the young racer for greatness, informed him less than one week after his victory that they would back out of the cash-intensive Superbike class due to a slowdown in sales. Rainey was bailed out by former racer Kenny Roberts, who was heading up Yamaha's 250-cc Grand Prix program, but the opportunity was too much too soon, and he struggled through the year with a top finish of third place, ending the 1984 season in eighth overall.

After dueling with rival Kevin Schwantz in 1987, Rainey eventually won another Superbike championship for Honda, and he campaigned at motorcycle racing's top level in 1990 in Yamaha's 500-cc Grand Prix class. So hungry was Rainey for success that when he finally captured the championship at the end of the season, he later said, "When I crossed the line and I was World Champion, I had this burst of emotion. I felt great, for about two tenths of a second," he added, "then it was gone. It left me feeling really disappointed." Rainey would cap off three consecutive 500-cc Grand Prix championships by 1992 and fight harder than ever during the 1993 season. He

Wayne Rainey's 1983 Superbike was donated to the Motorcycle Hall of Fame Museum by Kawasaki.

Wayne Rainey approaching full lean on his Kawasaki.
Courtesy the Motorcycle Hall of Fame Museum

was enjoying a healthy points lead at the Italian GP at Misano when tragedy struck 10 laps into the race. Entering a 130-mile-per-hour right-hand turn, he lost control and skidded across the tarmac and onto the gravel trap, sustaining back injuries that would paralyze him permanently from the chest down. Stripped of his ability to walk and the prospect of continuing in the field into which he had poured his life's passion, Rainey abandoned racing with a second-place finish for the 1993 GP season, returning in 1994 to coach Yamaha's factory Grand Prix team for four years before retiring in 1998.

Rainey's 1983 Superbike championship–winning No. 60 Kawasaki propelled his career toward a record that would include two world Superbike championships (and the second highest number of career Superbike wins ever), 64 podium finishes and 24 wins in 500-cc GP racing, and three GP world championships. Though his career was prematurely cut short, Wayne Rainey is widely considered to be one of racing's greatest competitors. By exhibiting his raw skill on a bike underequipped for the task at hand, he proved that sometimes a rise to greatness can result when the will to succeed meets the right opportunity.

Above: The technology of the Kawasaki's air-cooled engine lagged behind that of its water-cooled competitors.

Left: A hand-painted script identifies Rainey's bike.

12

COLIN EDWARDS'

YAMAHA TZ250D

The Bike That Launched a Career

Colin Edwards got a considerable head start on racing. As a toddler, he would wander to the garage and perch on his father's supercharged Honda 750. By age 3, he was racing dirt bikes, and at 7 he scored his first contract. Edwards continued to dominate amateur racing until he became burned out at the tender age of 14 and finally called it quits. "It was just a job," he later said. "I'd had enough."

However, external forces were at play while Edwards resumed his adolescence. His father, a former amateur racer who still felt the allure of the track, was buying and selling cars when he acquired a repossessed Yamaha FZR1000. "Here I am, sixteen years old, with access to an FZR1000," Edwards recalls. "My dad had a sly, coy little plan." On his birthday, his father bought him a Kawasaki ZX-7 (which Edwards jokingly suspects was put on a 50-year finance plan), then invited him to watch a road race.

When Edwards saw Jeff Covington—whom he had regularly beaten in motocross—win, he knew he was easily faster than every competitor in

Opposite: Colin Edwards on his No. 45 Yamaha TZ250D during the 1992 season. *Tom Halverson*

the race. A couple weeks later, Edwards squeezed into his mother's 1970s orange-and-black Bates leathers and put in a few laps at a track. When he finally asked his father if he could pursue road racing, his dad responded enthusiastically, "Hell yeah, we can do it!"

Edwards took up endurance racing on FZR400s, and at a Grand National final event in Atlanta, he happened to run into Tom Halverson, who had worked on his bikes during Edwards' three years in motocross with Yamaha. Halverson's advice to the newly indoctrinated road racer was to "get on a TZ250; it's a purpose-built racer that will help you develop skills that streetbikes won't."

At the age of 17, a newly invigorated Edwards rode a Honda 600, an RC30, and a Yamaha TZ250—racking up more seat time in a season than ever before, or since. He took a record five national titles in the AMA/CCS Race of Champions at Daytona, as well as a record eight national titles in the WERA/GNF meeting at Road Atlanta.

Just before the 1992 season, he picked up a South West Motorsports Yamaha sponsorship in the AMA 250-cc Nationals. That series was considered a stepping stone to Superbike racing, and in order to maximize the opportunity presented to him, Edwards had to quickly get up to speed on his nimble No. 45 Yamaha TZ250D. Fortunately, the years of experience riding two-strokes familiarized him with the Yamaha. The bike's V-twin configuration, which was a departure from earlier parallel-twin designs, produced less vibration, enabling a smaller and lighter chassis and a weight of only 217 pounds.

His bike demanded finesse and accuracy, which Edwards exhibited when he won the first race of the season at Daytona. His quick ascension in road racing, however, hit several speed bumps: While riding at a WERA race, he blew out both anterior cruciate ligaments (ACLs) in his knees, and a front brake failure at Texas World Speedway threw him into the Armco, breaking his wrist. Ignoring these injuries and focusing on the season, Edwards battled future 500-cc Grand Prix champion Kenny Roberts Jr. in what would be considered one of the most competitive 250-cc series ever. After winning five out of nine races, Edwards became the 1992 AMA 250-cc Grand Prix champion, an auspicious debut enabling him to join Yamaha's Vance & Hines Factory AMA Superbike team the following year. He won three AMA Superbike events in his first season and was recruited to Yamaha's Factory World Superbike team for the second season.

Edwards went on to win the World Superbike championship in 2000 and 2002, and he joined MotoGP racing in 2003 under the Aprilia banner. He raced for Honda Telefonica in 2004 and finished the season in sixth, the highest position for any MotoGP racer coming from Superbike.

The Yamaha's V-twin configuration produces less vibration than its predecessor, allowing for a lighter, more compact chassis.

He then raced for Yamaha's GP team in 2005 and 2006, serving as teammate to seven-time world champion Valentino Rossi.

Thanks to a professional racing debut aboard his No. 45 Yamaha during the 1992 season, Colin Edwards earned the nickname "Texas Tornado." When discussing the season in which he joined the ranks of pro road racing and launched his remarkable career, Edwards attributes his success to his willingness—while suggesting that naïveté may have also figured in the equation. "I was young, dumb, full of piss and vinegar, and ready to go," he says, emphasizing that it was perhaps his ignorance of the caliber of his competitors that allowed him to perform without intimidation. The drive exhibited during his breakthrough performance typifies the ambitious spirit that carried Colin Edwards to the top class of motorcycle racing and will perhaps take him even further.

One of the two carbon-fiber exhaust silencers on the Yamaha.

13

LEO PAYNE'S
TURNIP EATER

The 200-mile-per-hour Hog

Leo Payne was a devoted Harley enthusiast with a strange conundrum: though he had an undeniable attraction to the laid-back American bikes, he also loved speed. So in 1957, when he saw the new smaller and lighter Sportster model at friend Mike Wilson's dealership, Payne was fascinated. He had owned several Harleys (including his first bike, a 125-cc model that he bought when he was 19), but this one was different. "He begged me to let him ride it," Wilson recalls, "but I explained to him that I had to sell it to somebody."

That "somebody" eventually turned out to be Payne. Because the Harley club in his hometown of Cedar Rapids, Iowa, consisted mostly of older, married couples, he would ride his Sportster with the Limey Club, an edgier group of enthusiasts who souped up Triumphs and BSAs. With one foot in the British bike scene and another in his definitively American machine, Payne's attraction to his Sportster would only strengthen, and he began modifying and racing the bike for a period that would span almost 20 years.

Opposite: Leo Payne on the *Turnip Eater* at the Bonneville Salt Flats. *Mike Wilson*
Above: The *Turnip Eater* at speed. *Mike Wilson*

One of the many
configurations in
which the *Turnip
Eater* competed at
Bonneville.
Mike Wilson

Mike Wilson was like a big brother to Payne, and he assisted him by modifying the engine cylinders and boring out the Likert carburetor to produce more horsepower. Payne, who had already accumulated hands-on experience working at a Harley dealership,immersed himself in the task of making the bike go obscenely fast. Before long, he became an expert at rebuilding race carburetors, a side business that garnered the attention of George Smith Sr., founder of the aftermarket motorcycle performance company S&S. Smith, who had pioneered the use of alcohol and nitromethane fuel, collaborated with Payne, and their continued innovations enabled his bike to dominate local and national drag strips for nearly a decade, where the *Turnip Eater* earned its name for beating countless British bikes.

Intent on maximizing the performance of the Sportster's iron-head V-twin, Payne bore its cylinders to 1,500 cc, squeezing 9-second quarter-miles from the bike. He became obsessive about

Leo Payne sits on the
Turnip Eater in the
bed of a truck.
Mike Wilson

reducing the weight of its components, removing unnecessary parts, and shaving off extra metal. Wilson assisted Payne, often advising him not to pare the bike down too aggressively. "I would get on Leo for cutting down parts and making them too light," he says, emphasizing that structural integrity was more important than ultimate weight reduction. While the Harley's weight eventually dropped below 300 pounds, Payne also aided the bike's aerodynamics by incorporating a fairing from a Harley-Davidson Sprint. The bodywork suited the purpose ideally—it minimized frontal surface area, and Payne's diminutive 125-pound frame tucked tidily behind the shell.

Under the tutelage of Wilson, Payne began innovating new ways to maximize the capabilities of his machine. He was one of the first to perform burnouts before a race, a ritual that not only warmed the rear tire, but also had the side effect of intimidating his opponents. In keeping with his theme of weight loss, Payne incorporated a single-speed transmission and a clutch with ceramic pressure plates, the combination of which required skillful takeoffs. Payne enjoyed countless race wins throughout the 1960s, but the days of milking every ounce of performance out of his nitromethane-burning bike were coming to a head. By 1969—the year a new film called *Easy Rider* idealized the archetypal lifestyle of Harley-cruising hippies—Payne set his sights on a new frontier: the land-speed record.

In order to achieve his new goal, Payne teamed up with fellow Sportster fanatic Carl Morrow to repurpose the *Turnip Eater*'s configuration. At Bonneville, Payne incorporated his own fuel injection on an engine from Carl's Speed Shop, and the single gear setup meant that he had to hold onto a car door handle in order to reach approximately 75 miles per hour. It wasn't the most sophisticated approach, but it worked; slipping the clutch until he achieved approximately 110 miles per hour, Payne kept accelerating until he hit terminal velocity.

Leo Payne holds a conversation while awaiting tech inspection before his record-breaking 1970 run. *Mike Wilson*

Leo Payne's *Turnip Eater* was restored by Mike Wilson to the configuration in which it averaged 202.379 miles per hour at Bonneville in 1970.

Payne managed to achieve an astonishing one-way trap speed of 222 miles per hour, but engine failure prevented him from creating a record. By subsequently installing a second motor, he achieved a trap speed of 201 miles per hour on one of two successful runs, making Payne the first rider to achieve over 200 miles per hour in a non-streamlined motorcycle. However, his average speed was calculated at 196,512 miles per hour, and while he broke the existing class record by an incredible 43 miles per hour, the run was not technically a land-speed record. Undaunted, he returned to Bonneville in 1970 to take another stab. The *Turnip Eater*, wearing a road race fairing from a Harley XRTT, eventually produced an average speed of 202.379, officially breaking the 200-mile-per-hour barrier.

Though Payne proved to himself and the racing community that he could master both the drag strip and the salt flats, he insisted on competing with the *Turnip Eater* until he retired in the mid-1970s. Payne passed away in 1992 after consistently redefining the boundaries of his machine's performance; by competing with the same motorcycle over the course of almost 20 years, he proved that a racer didn't necessarily need a new bike in order to break new ground and remain competitive.

Shortly before his death, Payne asked Wilson—who had sold him the *Turnip Eater* 34 years earlier—to take care of the bike and ensure that it would not be raced or ridden. In honor of Payne's and the bike's most famous accomplishment—the land-speed record—Wilson restored

the bike to the same state in which it ran at Bonneville and donated it to the Motorcycle Hall of Fame Museum.

Sometimes, in the hands of the right person, a motorcycle can be modified and improved to accomplish groundbreaking performances that belie its ancient technology. Tuner, drag racer, and top-speed rider Leo Payne did exactly that with his *Turnip Eater*. As a member of the 200-mile-per-hour club and numerous other accolades earned during its considerable lifespan, the *Turnip Eater* remains a testament to the power of innovative thinking, and the American ingenuity that can turn an innocuous V-twin-powered Harley into a nitromethane-burning record breaker.

Payne was responsible for numerous custom modifications to the *Turnip Eater*, including this fairing, which accommodated the carburetor intake.

Left: Only the bare essentials—and a cheeky graphic on the tank—characterize the view from the *Turnip Eater*'s cockpit.

14

T. E. LAWRENCE'S
BROUGH SUPERIOR SS100

Lawrence of Arabia's Last Ride

David Lean's *Lawrence of Arabia* dedicates over three hours to gorgeously shot vistas and desert landscapes while depicting T. E. Lawrence's epic exploits as a lieutenant during World War I, but the 1962 film begins on a personal note. During the opening credits, Lawrence's character, played by Peter O'Toole, quietly prepares his Brough Superior SS100 for a ride. Kick-starting the fierce soundtrack of the 998-cc V-twin JAP motor, Lawrence accelerates and becomes at one with his machine and the road. The scene is an understated introduction to the enigmatic military and literary icon who became famous for aiding the British cause by coordinating Arab revolts in the Middle East. After the war, as he settled into civilian life, Lawrence became increasingly passionate about the meditative practice of enjoying fast motorcycles in the idyllic British countryside.

"A skittish motor bike with a touch of blood in it," Lawrence wrote in *The Road,* his treatise on the speed and satisfaction derived from

Opposite: T. E. Lawrence astride *George VII*, the Brough Superior on which he would experience his fatal crash.

motorcycling, "is better than all the riding animals on earth, because of its logical extension of our faculties, and the hint, the provocations, to excess conferred by its honeyed, untiring smoothness." Brough Superior, Lawrence's bike of choice, boasted an amalgamation of the best parts available at any cost and used the tagline "The Rolls-Royces of Motorcycles" in its ads, a claim that went uncontested from the notoriously sensitive carmaker. Lawrence's love affair with the brand began in 1922 with the purchase of his first Brough Superior, a Mark 1 model nicknamed *George I* (his subsequent Broughs would be named *George II*, *George III*, etc). Lawrence would eventually buy a total of seven Broughs, referring to them all as "Boanerges" (or "Boa"), a name of Biblical origin that means "sons of thunder." The impetuous nickname referred to the bikes' high-strung temperament, and during the latter portion of Lawrence's life, the bikes offered him a visceral form of escape, simultaneously feeding his imagination and satisfying his wanderlust.

A front view of
George VII.
Lawrence's goggles
are wrapped around
the windscreen.

Lawrence's first bike was purchased following the publication of *The Seven Pillars of Wisdom*, and it cemented an addiction that would seal his untimely fate with *George VII*, a Brough Superior SS100 that he obtained in 1932 at the cost of £170. As with all Brough Superiors, Lawrence's last bike was bespoke, fitted to his 5-foot, 5½-inch frame. SS100 models were each personally certified by George Brough to be capable of 100 miles per hour, and Lawrence—a connoisseur of velocity as well as style—wrote a letter of appreciation to Brough in September 1926: "Yesterday I completed 100,000 miles, since 1922, on five successive Brough Superiors . . . thank you for the road-pleasure I have got out of them . . . your present machines are as fast and reliable as express trains, and the greatest fun in the world to drive: and I say this after twenty years experience of cycles and cars." In Lawrence's estimation, he often logged 500 miles a day—and sometimes 700—on his Brough, traversing back roads solely for the pleasure of riding, if nothing else.

George VII—T. E. Lawrence's seventh and final motorcycle, engine number 22000/S, frame number 1041.S—was ridden regularly and outfitted with some of the best equipment of its time, including a Bentley & Draper rear suspension system and Castle Brampton front forks. In another letter to Brough, Lawrence—under the pseudonym of T. E. Shaw (a moniker he morphed from his friend George Bernard Shaw)—wrote of his Boa, "It is the silkiest thing I have ever ridden: partly because of the perfect tune, partly from the high gear . . . I think this is going to be a very excellent bike. The crowds that gape at her, just now, will stop looking after she gets dirty . . . I am very grateful to you and everybody for the care taken to make her perfect."

After clocking over 25,000 miles on his Brough, on May 13, 1935, Lawrence was riding through Egdon Heath from Bovington Army Camp in Dorset toward his Clouds Hill cottage when he collided with a bicycle being ridden by Burt Hargreaves, who was riding alongside his

After T. E. Lawrence's accident, his Brough Superior was stored at the service bay on the right.

friend. Lawrence, having been thrown from his motorcycle, suffered a 9-inch gash to his head and lay bleeding by the side of the road until he was picked up by an army truck. He was comatose for six days at Bovington Camp Hospital before succumbing to his injuries on May 19, 1935.

Burt Hargreaves' bicycle, which was struck by Lawrence's motorcycle.

On May 21, the day of Lawrence's funeral, coroner Ralph Neville Jones held an inquest and examined the damaged Brough. A few of his findings contradicted the depiction of the crash in the opening sequence of *Lawrence of Arabia*; based on the damage to the motorcycle and the bicycle, it appeared the cyclists were traveling in the same direction as Lawrence (the film portrays them as riding toward him). Also, the damage to the bicycle's rear wheel suggests that the bike was turning during the moment of impact, which is contrary to the boys' sworn statements—they

T. E. Lawrence's Brough Superior was held as evidence for the coroner's inquest and is seen here on a Ford Model T on May 21, 1935, the day of Lawrence's funeral. Note the visible license plate.

said they were traveling single file, straight down the road. Additionally, the registration number on the motorcycle in the film, UL 656, was actually that of *George VI*, the bike that preceded Lawrence's final bike, the plates of which actually read GW 2275.

After the accident, the motorcycle was stored for three months at the garage where it had been serviced. Lawrence's brother Arnold declined George Brough's offer to rebuild the damaged motorcycle for £40—a considerable amount in 1935—choosing instead to sell the bike back to him. The damage to the motorcycle included a bent kick-starter and footpegs, a grazed saddle, the loss of the headlamp rim, and a dent in the fuel tank from the impacted shift lever. The stainless-steel tank, which T. E. Lawrence had replaced three months prior to the accident, was refitted by Brough with a traditional chromium-plated tank and painted black by a subsequent owner. To this day, traces of damage to the handlebar and the front mudguard remain visible. George Brough would eventually sell the mostly repaired motorcycle to a Cambridge dealership, which placed the bike in its window display for publicity.

T. E. Lawrence's final Brough Superior eventually traded hands until it found its seventh and current owner. The owner, who wishes not to be identified, is the first person since Lawrence to own all the memorabilia associated with the motorcycle, including Lawrence's goggles, the bike's original log book, its 1935 tax disc (indicating that it was paid up for road use), and a pair of brass fuel filters (with Lawrence's currency still inside).

Arguably the most famous road-going motorcycle of all time, T. E. Lawrence's last bike is currently on display at London's Imperial War Museum and exists as the only surviving motorcycle that can be positively identified as his. In contrast to the heroic military campaigns in which T. E. Lawrence seemed impervious to harm, the 1932 Brough Superior SS100 speaks as much to his enthusiasm for riding as it does to his fragile mortality.

Peter O'Toole astride T. E. Lawrence's last bike. O'Toole's performance in *Lawrence of Arabia* launched his career.

15

ELVIS PRESLEY'S

HARLEY-DAVIDSON ELECTRA-GLIDE

A Ride Fit for the King

Born in a tiny house in Tupelo, Mississippi, to a truck driver and a seamstress, The King grew up in conditions that were anything but regal. Elvis Aaron Presley was deprived of life's luxuries, but those limitations would become a hidden blessing. At the age of 11, when his wish for a bicycle went unfulfilled, his mother gave him a $13 guitar instead. This gift triggered an awakening of Elvis' innate singing talent, and he signed with Sun Records in 1955.

Presley became a motorcycle enthusiast as soon as his finances permitted. Upon earning his first advance from Sun Records, he purchased a 125-cc Harley Hummer, which was maintained by local mechanic and future tuner Jerry Branch. When Presley earned a bonus for switching to RCA Records, he graduated from the diminutive Hummer to a larger, 883-cc 1956 Harley-Davidson Model K. His reputation as a dyed-in-the-wool Hog fan became established when he and the bike appeared on the May 1956 cover of the Harley-Davidson publication *Enthusiast*.

Opposite: Elvis, in what appears to be a moment of contemplation, was actually looking into the empty fuel tank of his 1956 Harley-Davidson Model K. *© Alfred Wertheimer/photokunst*

Elvis' 1976 Harley-Davidson Electra-Glide typified his taste in motorcycles; it was large, commanding, and low to the ground.

As Elvis' blues-influenced rock 'n' roll exploded in popularity, he became notorious for scandalously suggestive onstage gyrations. His moves were so controversial that cameramen were instructed to frame him from the waist up when he appeared on Ed Sullivan's "Talk of the Town" TV show. An insinuation of rebelliousness became part of his public persona, but film studios were skittish about featuring protagonists with an unsavory edge. So in the 1964 Paramount Pictures release *Roustabout*, Elvis rode an innocuous Honda 350 Superhawk, a choice which sought to place him in the demographic idealized by the manufacturer's famous slogan: "You meet the nicest people on a Honda." While Triumphs and Hondas would eventually share garage space with his Harleys, it was the American brand that would remain synonymous with Elvis' charismatic personality. Though his career slowed during the mid-1960s, the black leathers Elvis wore during his 1968 comeback concert recalled the bad-boy image sported by Marlon Brando in *The Wild One* and reasserted Presley's authentic style.

As his career grew, Elvis' enthusiasm for motorcycles and cars proved unselfish; he often bestowed friends, family, and business associates with two- and four-wheeled gifts. His local entourage—known as the "Memphis Mafia"—were frequent recipients of his generosity, and they enjoyed riding with Presley regardless of weather or time of day. His choice in bikes was independent of their cost, as Memphis Mafia member Joe Esposito describes it: "It didn't matter if it cost a million dollars and another cost a dime," he explained. "If he liked it, he would pick the one that cost a dime." Though Presley's tastes ran the gamut, he had a soft spot for traditional Harley-Davidson dressers. "He loved Harleys that were big and close to the ground," explains Ron Elliot, who maintained Elvis' fleet of bikes.

Presley's bike purchases were often impulsive, as evidenced by a certain Harley-Davidson Electra-Glide. Following a series of concerts in Fayetteville, North Carolina, in August 1976, he stopped in Memphis before heading to his Palm Springs home. While in Palm Springs, he purchased a 1976 Electra-Glide on August 11 and headed to San Antonio, Texas, on August 26 for more performances. The Harley was painted Elvis blue with stenciled gear sprockets, creating a subtle pattern on the saddlebags and tank.

During the 1970s, Elvis' career would peak and begin a steady decline. He experienced depression following his divorce from Priscilla Presley. His global stardom enabled him to fulfill every stereotype of rock star excess, and he battled an addiction to prescription drugs, struggled with weight gain, and suffered from spiraling health problems. Nonetheless, he toured heavily and, between 1968 and 1977, put in over 1,100 performances, most of which were before sold-out audiences.

The Harley's 1,200-cc V-twin produces massive torque.

The Electra-Glide's paint features a unique pattern created by the use of gear sprockets as stencils.

A copy of the DMV registration attributing the bike to Elvis Presley.

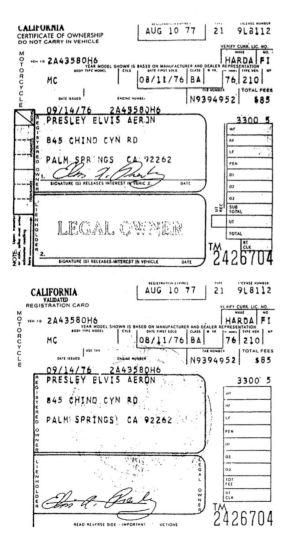

While Elvis Presley's career ebbed and flowed—going into and out of varying degrees of revolution, trend setting, and alternatively stasis and hibernation—motorcycles were a constant fixture. A symbol of escape, freedom, and ultimate independence, in many ways, bikes represented to Elvis the same qualities his music represented to a generation.

The blue Electra-Glide Elvis purchased in August 1976 is one of the rare Elvis-owned motorcycles not on display at Graceland, and few details are known about its history. David Geisler, a collector who operates the Pioneer Auto Show in Murdo, South Dakota, traded several cars for Elvis' Harley in 1982. The bike is currently on display there among over 250 vintage cars and motorcycles.

The bikes on permanent display in Graceland include a 1966 Harley chopper, a 1976 Electra-Glide 1200 Liberty, a Bicentennial Edition 1976 Electra-Glide, and a 1965 Honda Dream. It is a testament to the motorcycle culture perpetuated by Elvis' legacy that, in 2007, a Harley-Davidson dealership opened at the Graceland visitor center.

As homegrown as the Harleys he rode, Elvis combined defiance with charming accessibility. This concept of accessible rebelliousness redefined not only what the public accepted but what it considered American.

The bikes on permanent display in Graceland include a 1966 Harley chopper, a 1976 Electra-Glide 1200 Liberty, a Bicentennial Edition 1976 Electra-Glide, and a 1965 Honda Dream.

16

JOHN BRITTEN'S

BRITTEN V-1000

The Modern Masterpiece

For insight into the outlandishly sculpted, shockingly innovative Britten V-1000 race bike, one must consider the brief life and times of John Britten, the mind behind the motorcycle.

The seeds of Britten's gifts were visible early on; as a kid with a talent for tinkering, he improvised the construction of go-karts, and by age 13, he and a friend had restored an abandoned Indian Scout.

In spite of his dyslexia, Britten enrolled in a mechanical engineering course after attending St. Andrew's College, working as a draftsman before designing a highway project in England. Though the work was well suited to his technical proficiency, Britten's career took a turn in 1976 when, at the age of 26, he shifted his focus to fine art. Newly committed to crafting handmade glass lighting fixtures, he indulged deeply in his creativity, which had previously taken a back seat to nuts-and-bolts

Opposite: The Britten V-1000's unmistakable stance resembles no other bike. Its unique pink-and-blue paint job was inspired by the colors of a starfish-shaped piece of handblown glass Britten brought from Australia.

practicality. "You're more likely to succeed if you choose what you want to design," Britten would later say, recalling the individualist attitude that would become an overarching theme of his work.

Concurrent with his budding creativity was a burgeoning passion for racing motorcycles. In 1986, Britten started with a bevel-drive Ducati Darmah racer—a bike that exuded personality but lacked reliability—and began with some simple improvements. For the person who successfully converted a neglected Victorian-style stable into an art nouveau–inspired home, building a better bike seemed eminently feasible.

National pride is integrated into the Britten's design: four red stars on the Britten's blue tank reference the New Zealand flag.

Britten began tweaking the Ducati powerplant, but his pet project eventually morphed into a trellis-framed, Denco-powered methanol burner sporting a fabricated aluminum swingarm. The radical mechanical makeover was housed in a handmade carbon-fiber monocoque chassis wrapped in sleek, aerodynamically slippery bodywork. The iterations of the bikes—which would later be referred to as the AERO-D-Zero and the AERO-D-One—ended up winning the 1987 BEARS (British, European, American Racing Series) speed trials, clocking at 148.21 miles per hour.

Eager to improve upon the AERO series, Britten set out to build an even more advanced race bike using state-of-the-art techniques such as hand-forming carbon fiber, as well as a few primitive but inventive ones (including baking a prototype 1000-cc V-twin powerplant in a backyard kiln.)

Industrial designer Shaun Craill would later say of Britten, "He didn't understand he was being unconventional because he hadn't been taught what conventional design was." The exuberance of Britten's unfettered creativity was made shockingly clear with his new creation, the V-1000. Wild, futuristic, and dynamic, the bike's design merged hand-crafted carbon-fiber/Kevlar composite bodywork, which incorporated Britten's unique "skin and bones" construction technique, with the stunning beauty of its exposed mechanical workings. From the ground up, the bike represented Britten's vision of an uncompromising racer.

In keeping with the bike's sparse functionality, the V-1000 seat consists of two small pads fitted snugly within the bodywork.

Without the extensive bodywork of his earlier bikes (which hampered access to the engine), the V-1000 gains its aerodynamic advantage by minimizing frontal surface area. The V-twin configuration was chosen for its relatively narrow profile (thereby reducing drag), and the powerplant is preceded with a fairing possessing two thin, horizontal slits routing air to an under-seat radiator (again, minimizing frontal surface area).

Because it lacks a conventional frame, the bike's innards appear to be suspended midair. Incorporating a novel setup in

The V-1000's aluminum exhaust silencers produce a deep but muted bass sound, and its underseat radiator is notorious for heating up the thin seat.

which the tops of the cylinders are connected to the saddle via a beam, the V-1000's structure centers around the engine—both figuratively and literally. The rear suspension is mounted to the front of the engine via a carbon-fiber swingarm with an adjustable linkage, and the front forks are of a girder-style carbon construction, seemingly retro in form but in fact quite modern in function. Lighter than traditional upside-down telescopic forks, Britten's girder design combats brake dive without completely eliminating feel, allowing for some compression during braking. Adjustable mounts enable relatively soft spring and damping, while permitting control over rake, trail, and wishbone settings. In Britten's words, the setup is "a girder parallelogram, semi-intelligent front suspension, which is much more sophisticated than a conventional motorbike in that it can differentiate between a brake or a bump force."

While the V-1000's components are remarkably lightweight, the sand-cast aluminum-alloy engine case is relatively heavy due to its role as a central stressed unit. Developed with the assistance of renowned tuner Jerry Branch, the V-1000 powerplant cantilevers pressure created by high g-force riding and is engineered to perform reliably against the brutal rigors of racing (though its high tolerances and tremendous piston velocities require the engine to be disassembled and inspected after five cumulative hours of running). The cylinders of Britten's liquid-cooled V-1000 powerplant are configured at 60 degrees, fed by two sequential Bosch fuel injectors per cylinder that can be tuned with a laptop computer. The engine is blueprinted so well that it produces a silky-smooth 165 horsepower at 12,400 rpm without the aid of counterbalancers.

By 1991, John Britten's underdog motorcycle hit the circuits and scored an amazing second and third against factory machines at Daytona's Battle of the Twins competition. At Daytona in 1992, Andrew Stroud, riding a V-1000, egged Ducati rider Pascal Picotte on with wheelstands and passes, until a crossed battery wire forced him to fall behind in the second-to-last lap. Britten would later lament that it "serve[d] him right for using a Ducati part," a statement that reinforced his homegrown, do-it-yourself attitude.

The V-1000 would go on to set world speed and acceleration records and win numerous races, emerging victorious in 1995's BEARS. More significant, however, was the singular

John Britten experimented with different handmade exhaust routings, and Virgil Elings' bike features a less convoluted version.

vision with which the bike was conceived and executed. Essentially the first prototype motorcycle to achieve consistent race success, the V-1000 could not have come to fruition without the ambitious vision of its creator. Britten seemed to lack limitations—both creatively and inspirationally—that might prevent him from achieving a functionally superior and aesthetically beautiful race bike. His brilliant career came to a sudden halt, however, when, shortly after his 45th birthday, Britten died of melanoma. While six V-1000s were completed during his lifetime, his vision of building a total of 10 V-1000 motorcycles would be completed posthumously, and the final bike was shipped in February 1999, four years after his death.

The last Britten was owned by Michael Iannuccilli of Las Vegas until it was sold to Virgil Elings, who displays it at his Vintage Motorcycle Museum in Solvang, California. The bike—which spent most of its life crated (with the exception of a ride by Jason McEwan at a Britten memorial event)—was never raced. It was delivered to Mr. Elings on brand-new slicks and lapped by him at Willow Springs, where he reached 10,000 rpm in top gear on the track's notoriously fast straightaway. Elings recalls thinking, "Don't. Even. Do. This," as he approached terminal velocity.

Lightweight but strong carbon fiber was incorporated liberally throughout the bike, including the swingarm and the wheels.

A rare example of functionality married with beauty, the V-1000 is widely considered one of the great landmark race motorcycles of the twentieth century. The arc of John Britten's life may have been short, but as evidenced by the V-1000—his groundbreaking masterpiece—it was touched with a gift of exceptional brilliance.

17

EVEL KNIEVEL'S
HARLEY-DAVIDSONS

The Original Daredevil's Chariots of Choice

In the rough-and-tumble copper mining town of Butte, Montana, during the late 1950s, a young Robert Craig Knievel struggled to make a name for himself. Having dabbled in crime and worked odd jobs as a miner, a hunting guide, and a motorcycle salesman, Knievel realized that he needed to pick a vocation that, as he described it, "put a lump in my throat and a knot in my stomach." Though he started motorcycle racing after his father bought him a BSA 125, he found his true calling when he formed the Evel Knievel Motorcycle Daredevils in 1965.

Jumping his Honda scrambler over rattlesnakes and riding through flaming walls, Knievel thrived on the rush from his death-defying stunts. Inspired by the showmanship of Elvis Presley and Liberace, he injected a theatrical, almost gladiatorial element to his performances. His name started circulating, and his first appearance on ABC's Wide World of Sports in March 1967 offered him a taste of the tremendous power of television.

Opposite: An ardent supporter of helmet use, Evel once offered a cash reward for anyone who spotted him stunting without head protection. *Evel Knievel archives*

The jump that started it all: Knievel leaps over the fountains at Caesar's Palace, only to crash and remain in a coma for 29 days. *Evel Knievel archives*

On December 31 of that year, Knievel persuaded Jay Sarno, the owner of Caesar's Palace in Las Vegas, to allow him to jump the fountains outside the famous hotel. The ABC network, unconvinced of the stunt's ability to draw a sizable TV audience, agreed to air the footage later if it lived up to its spectacular promise. Knievel, confident the jump would be broadcast worthy, paid a crew to film the event.

After walking through the casino and losing $100 at a roulette table, Knievel took a shot of Wild Turkey and performed the bone-crushing 151-foot jump that would put him in a coma for 29 days and launch his career. Footage of his landing, which was replayed in slow motion, revealed Knievel separating from his Triumph and tumbling across the pavement; audiences were simultaneously shocked and fascinated by the man whose hubris sent him soaring across the sky on a bike. Though doctors told him he might not be able to walk again without crutches, Knievel returned to jumping in order to satiate his new national audience—and to cover his hospital bills. Several performances and more broken bones later, he became disenchanted with Triumph for not paying him to ride its bikes and signed a deal with American Eagle, a company that applied its nameplate to Italian Laverdas.

In late 1970, as American Eagle went out of business, Evel Knievel signed a new deal that would mark a milestone in the evolution of his image. Harley-Davidson provided bikes and a generous sponsorship deal for Knievel, whose renegade persona seemed perfectly matched to the manufacturer of "Great American Freedom Machines." His first jump on a Harley came on December 12, 1970, in Los Angeles, where he successfully cleared 13 cars at the Lions Drag Strip.

Finally, Knievel's notoriety allowed him to cash in on his success, and though painful injuries were a frequent result of his jumps, he enjoyed widespread recognition and traveled in an extravagantly customized 60-foot 18-wheeler. A telling plaque inside his truck displayed a quote from Robert Frost: "The people I want to hear about are the people who take risks."

The new Harley-Davidsons, on which he would perform several of his most famous jumps, began as stock dirt trackers. In 1970, while professional racers were waiting to get their hands on the highly anticipated aluminum-engine XR750s—which replaced the archaic iron-barrel version—Knievel was provided with three: one for jumps, another for wheelies, and a spare. He hired three-time Daytona 200 winner Roger Reiman to modify the bikes for jumping, a function dramatically different from their original purpose. The minimal wheel travel of the stock XR750 made it poorly suited to the task of hard landings, so Reiman installed a heavier-duty front end with thicker shock absorber oil and heavier shocks at the rear. When wheel spokes broke during one of Knievel's test jumps, heavier-duty rods were installed.

In spite of its suspension reinforcements, the 300-pound bike created considerable compression upon landing. The rear shocks were known to completely bottom out when they hit the ground first, and though the Harley was not meant to land on its front wheel, when it did, its shock seals tended to blow. Because trackers were not traditionally equipped with brakes, Reiman retrofitted Evel's Harleys with front and rear drum units taken from late 1960s Sportsters. Adding

Evel Knievel's leathers—which offered minimal crash protection—featured Confederate flag–style graphics. *Evel Knievel archives*

Below: Knievel's crash at Wembley Stadium before 90,000 fans; shortly after being helped up, he announced his retirement. *Evel Knievel archives*

a touch of showmanship and occasion to each event, the Harley's tanks were painted with themes that corresponded to the jump, and unlike traditionally functional dirt trackers, the bike's metal parts were chromed.

Evel enjoyed his association with Harley-Davidsons not only because their style suited him but also because of their crowd-pleasing exhaust roar and the wheelie-popping torque produced by their V-twin powerplants. Though he had no specific prejump ritual, friend Earl Castine remembers Knievel carrying a lucky rabbit's foot, and that in the hours leading up to the main event, Evel "psyched himself up by changing his personality; he'd get on edge a couple hours before he was going to jump." In practice runs, Knievel rode toward the ramp, experimenting with different speeds, veering away at the last moment to get a sense of what kind of takeoff velocity he would need. His Harleys lacked speedometers and tachometers, and Knievel flew by the seat of his pants, trusting the sound of the engine rather than distracting himself with gauges.

He hated the idea of unnecessary gear shifts as he approached the takeoff ramp, so Reiman installed crankshaft sprockets that, depending on the ramp length, allowed the bike to always leave the ground in second gear. Evel equipped his motorcycles with parachutes (which were emblazoned with the lucky horseshoe logo of one of his sponsors, Olympia Beer), but one midair deployment during a demo in Atlanta decelerated the bike so suddenly that he decided to only use it for show, after most of the speed was scrubbed off with his brakes. During another jump, the chute became entangled in his rear wheel, creating even less of an argument for the gimmick.

Knievel's Harley-Davidson XR750, which jumped at Wembley Stadium, King's Island, and Chicago, is displayed in his promotional trailer.

Knievel speaking at the 2006 "Days of Evel" festival in Butte, Montana. Due to his affliction with idiopathic pulmonary fibrosis, he traveled with an oxygen tank.

Knievel, whose popularity grew dramatically during the early 1970s, wore the Harley-Davidson No. 1 logo without irony; it was a shameless symbol of his assertion that he was at the top of his field, the real deal in a world of imitators. During an unscripted moment at one of his jumps, Knievel psyched up the crowd, rode up to the top of the ramp, and had friend Mike Draper pull the safety pin on the parachute, which meant he was ready to jump. However, this time he told Draper to keep the bike revved, and he walked to the announcer and asked for the microphone. "I knew there would be a day in my life when I'd be too scared to jump," he told the crowd, which had quickly quieted. "But tonight," he continued, "is not that night."

Knievel took his exploits a step further in 1974 by attempting to jump Utah's Snake River Canyon in a purpose-built, jet-powered rocket. The parachute deployed prematurely and smashed the rocket against the cliff's edge, but Knievel would have perished had his craft landed in the river's rushing waters.

In May 1975, Knievel drew a record audience of 90,000 people at Wembley Stadium and jumped 13 double-decker buses. Though he broke his pelvis upon landing and announced minutes later that he "would never, ever, ever jump again," his Harley's bent frame was replaced by Reiman in time for a comeback jump five months later at King's Island in Ohio. He outdid his prior effort by flying over 14 Greyhound buses, setting a record for the top-rated ABC Wide World of Sports program and commanding a 52 percent share of viewership.

Evel Knievel's final major stunt, in which he attempted to leap over a tank of live sharks in the Chicago Amphitheater, was performed in the winter of 1976. Cancelled after a botched practice run that injured a cameraman and broke both of Knievel's arms, the event's conclusion only furthered the mystique of his fearlessness.

Though Evel's ties with Harley were temporarily severed after an alleged confrontation with an associate involving a baseball bat, both ultimately benefited from each other's iconic brands. One of Knievel's Harley-Davidson XR750s was donated to the Smithsonian National Museum of

Evel often warmed up the crowd by popping wheelies as he rode past. *Evel Knievel archives*

American History. The bike jumped at Wembley, King's Island, and at his final performance was owned by Knievel until his death. Its dented tank was customized for the event with a depiction of a shark rising towards the Chicago skyline.

Evel broke 35 bones over his career—many of which he rebroke numerous times—a statistic observed by the Guinness Book of World Records. Though his life was punctuated with physical suffering, it was also lived without regret. Theodore Roosevelt's words—which Evel often quoted—elegantly captured his motivation: "Far better it is to dare mighty things, to win glorious triumphs even though checkered by failure, than to rank with those poor spirits who neither enjoy nor suffer much because they live in the gray twilight that knows neither victory nor defeat."

It is a testament to the veracity with which Evel Knievel lived by those words that thousands converge yearly upon his hometown of Butte, Montana, to pay tribute to the original daredevil.

Knievel's XR750 was painted by George Sedlack; this scene depicts his final major appearance, Chicago's shark jump.

18

VON DUTCH'S
ORIGINALS

Customizing as an Art Form

Pinstriper, mechanic, metal worker, and artist Kenneth Howard is reputed to have earned the nickname "Von Dutch" because he was "stubborn as a Dutchman," and there is no greater evidence of his headstrong personality than the unconventional vestiges of his life's work.

At the age of 15, Dutch was doing cleanup work at a motorcycle shop when he brought home a gas tank and, using brushes from his father's toolbox, pinstriped it in order to hide paint imperfections. His boss—incredulous that a teenager had performed the work—bet that the kid could not reproduce the job on another bike. Promptly losing the wager, he promoted Dutch to work as a pinstriper and painter, a discipline he performed nonchalantly and with virtually subconscious ease. The surly teenager started developing his razor-sharp skills, building his legend, and establishing his contribution to what would become known as the Kustom Kulture movement.

Opposite: Von Dutch standing over one of his favorite motorcycles, a 1941 Condor. *Bird Betts collection*

Dutch's signature winged eyeball etched onto the rocker box of Bird Betts' 1969 Harley-Davidson FLH Police Special.

Dutch's etched Harley-Davidson emblem.

By the early 1950s, Dutch began working at Bud Ekins' Sherman Oaks shop, where he painted, performed mechanical work, and built vehicles for film productions. "We worked alone with very little conversation," recalls Ekins. "We worked together beautifully." While the results of Dutch's striping were aesthetically pleasing, the purpose of his paintwork was generally functional; hastily prepped bodywork often produced visible traces of grinding marks in the Bondo beneath the paint finish, and Dutch's talents enabled such flaws to be hidden. The more popular his signature pinstriping jobs became, the more he would charge, and before long Dutch's rate doubled, then tripled, in efforts to drive clients away. However, his contrarian attitude only reinforced his mystique. Dutch was innately skilled at striping, but the practice was not his passion. "I'm a mechanic first," he was known to say. "If I had my way, I'd be a gunsmith. I like to make things out of metal, because metal is forever. When you paint something, how long does it last? A few years, and then it's gone!"

Dutch's attraction to the permanence of metal was visceral. His nephew, Bird Betts, once brought him a massive brass handle that fell from a door at the Stardust hotel in Las Vegas. "You'd never seen a happier guy," Bird recalls. "He said, 'I'll be able to make ten, twelve knives out of this!'"—which, in fact, he did. Other outlandish fabrications by Dutch would include roller skates with two-stroke motors, a steam-powered television set, and a coin-operated guillotine.

During the late 1970s, Bird asked Dutch to customize his 1969 Harley-Davidson FLH Police Special, which had been converted from a dresser to a chopper. When Dutch painted its fuel tanks with large, gorily bloodshot eyeballs, Bird found the design too crude for his tastes. Dutch subsequently complied by repainting it—a rare action that revealed his regard for Bird. The bike was painted, totaled, and rebuilt in the 1980s, and according to Bird, the 1990 work on his Harley makes the bike the last object ever painted and striped by Dutch. The Harley features delicately interwoven painted scrolls highlighting the front fender, tanks, and frame. The bike's rocker boxes, cam cover, belt guard, and engine case are etched in precise strokes depicting his winged eyeball and the Harley-Davidson logo, among other designs. The Harley now sees use only once a year: on Bird's birthday.

Dutch detested materialism and appeared to derive no pleasure from money. When commissioned to paint Earl Bruce's 1955 Mercedes-Benz 300SL Gullwing, for instance, he responded in a way that negated the pedigree and status of the exotic sports car. Dutch, in an all-night frenzy that involved 70 rolls of masking tape and the consumption of untold bottles of beer and wine, flamed the car in loud, undulating waves that crept across the Benz's classic curves. "Everybody got mad at me," he later said. "They thought I had desecrated a shrine!" The reaction was, no doubt, just what he was looking for.

Bird Betts' 1969 Harley-Davidson FLH Police Special, the last motorcycle pinstriped by Von Dutch.

Above: Von Dutch's heavily louvered BMW side hack.

Right: Dutch's "Bitza This and That" referred to the fact that his BMW's side hack was constructed from what was essentially scrap metal.

Friend Gene Brown describes Dutch as "a provoker. He couldn't help himself; it was in his nature. He had to prod people." His casual insolence fueled his lore, making it difficult to disseminate truth from fiction. For instance, when a Hell's Angels member handed over a Harley-Davidson frame for pin-striping, Dutch allegedly felt an inexplicable compulsion to saw it into equal pieces measuring exactly 5⅛ inches. Stringing the metal together, he handed the pile back and said, "Just take this stupid motorcycle and get out of here"—which supposedly led to a contract being taken out on his life. A lover of German culture and machinery, Dutch once pieced together motorcycle parts from a Harley XA shaft drive, a BMW transmission, a Guzzi front end, and a gas tank from a Honda Dream 305. At the heart of the puzzle-like bike was a Volkswagen powerplant, and the striped and chromed tank featured a shiny VW logo.

Another window into Dutch's Teutonic personal tastes is his BMW R60, the last bike he owned. Dutch's mechanical aptitude came in handy when he restored and integrated the BMW's side hack and added a headlight to the front, around which he painted wings. The headlight had become his signature after he crashed his friend Keenan Wynn's Harley and attempted to repair the dent by drilling an access hole into its nose. Dutch also rerouted the BMW's exhaust past the sidecar, and he personalized it by heavily louvering its side and installing a bubble canopy from a salvaged plane at the Santa Paula airport. The rear storage box was painted with "Bitza this and that," a phrase reflecting both the bike's piecemeal nature and its owner's appreciation for flippant wordplay. Other custom touches include wheel hubs etched with BMW's aeronautically inspired propeller logo. The BMW, along with many personal effects, including handmade knives, guns, and cannons, is owned by Bird, who pays homage to Dutch's memory with his "Uncle Dutch" line of jewelry.

Dutch also developed a fondness for a 1941 Condor motorcycle that was dropped off at his shop for customizing, and when the owner saw how much Dutch enjoyed riding it, the loan became open-ended. A model originally employed by the Swiss Army, the 580-cc Condor was a lower-priced alternative to a BMW and features a similar, horizontally opposed engine configuration. Like his BMW, the Condor's fuel tank is painted with a swoop and gold stripes laid down by Dutch's

Von Dutch's 1941 Condor, photographed in Santa Paula near where Dutch spent the last days of his life.

notoriously steady hand, accenting the bike's uncomplicated shape. The irregularity of the surface upon which the pinstripes are painted suggests that Dutch was bragging to the world of his skill—in his own artistically extravagant way. His appreciation for the bike's rarity was reflected when somebody offered to trade him a brand-new Harley for the Condor. "Show me another Condor," Dutch told him, "and I'll trade you." Not surprisinly, the Condor stayed in Dutch's possession.

The Condor's construction is dominated by purposeful minimalism and features interchangeable front and rear wheel hubs, a hinged rear fender to facilitate wheel changes, and a wide-mouthed fuel filler neck. Handmade, knurled-metal sleeves are mounted over the footpegs, and a leather Luger gun holster is attached to the rear of the bike. The motorcycle, which was in Dutch's possession while he lived out of a bus in the Santa Paula area, is now a part of Daniel Schoenewald's private col-

The toolkit for Dutch's Condor still emanates the smell of motor oil.

lection and sees regular use in the same hills where Dutch used to ride.

Troubled and antisocial, Dutch's life was marked with more than its share of personal difficulties and extended periods of isolation, but he appreciated the mechanical honesty of motorcycles. "He just didn't like people for the most part," explains Bird. "But if Dutch liked you, he gave you everything he had. He was much more comfortable with machinery and tools. Those were his loves."

In 1992, Von Dutch died of liver cirrhosis after a life of customizing, fabricating, and painting countless knives, guns, cars, and bikes. "I striped 15,000 motorcycles and 4,000 cars," he said in 1970, "[and] none of those are around today. They wrecked them as fast as I could paint them." However, a few of his iconoclastic gestures do remain. In the case of an intricately surfaced Harley-Davidson, a utilitarian but whimsical BMW, and a discreetly adorned Condor, Von Dutch's impeccably detailed motorcycles serve as elegiac evidence of a life that was both baffling and brilliant.

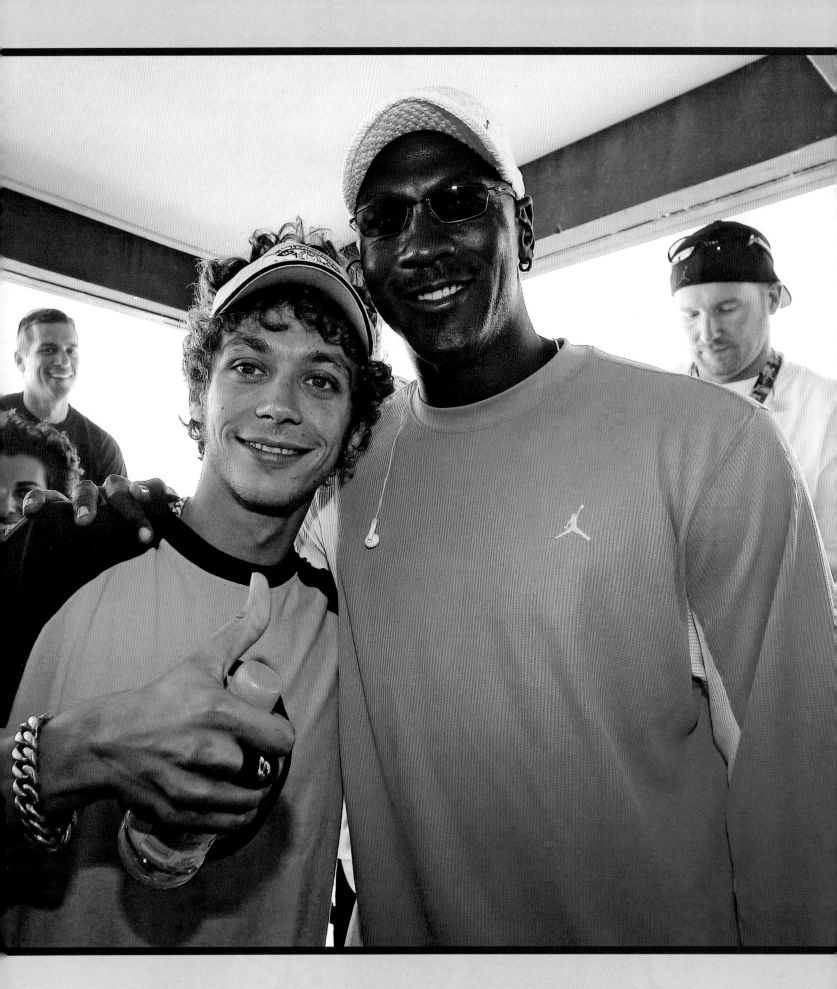

19

MICHAEL JORDAN'S
AMA RACING CONTENDERS

A Basketball Legend's Passion for Racing

It all started with a motorcycle ride one Sunday afternoon.

Michael Jordan—singular in his basketball achievements with six NBA Championships under his belt, 10 scoring titles, and the highest per-game points average in NBA history—was enjoying a ride in the spring of 2003 when he stopped for gas and started chatting with a group of sportbike riders. Discussing the finer points of high-performance riding (and lightly admonishing Jordan for his lack of protective gear), they eventually introduced the basketball legend to racer Montez Stewart, whom Jordan later assisted when the No Limits racing team experienced financial difficulties.

Jordan befriended Stewart, and after renting Blackhawk Farms Raceway for a day and outfitting himself with custom leathers, the retired basketball legend caught the racing bug. "It was the best day that I have had in a long time," Jordan later said. "I was learning from Montez . . . the guys started giving me what they knew about road racing, and I've been hooked ever since."

Opposite: Michael Jordan and Valentino Rossi following the 2005 Laguna Seca USGP.
Andrew Northcott

Steve Rapp wheelies from corner 11 at Mid-Ohio. *Brian J. Nelson*

MJ's motorcycling interests began with dirt biking at the age of five with his brothers in North Carolina, and those interests were stoked years later when his team presented coach Phil Jackson the gift of a Harley-Davidson following a championship victory. Because his NBA contract prohibited him from "dangerous" activities while competing, Jordan's desire to ride went unsatisfied. However, free to do as he chose after retirement, he found himself digging deeper into his passion for motorcycles.

Attracted to the discipline of racing, Jordan took his enthusiasm to its farthest possible edge: he decided to start an AMA race team under the banner of Michael Jordan Motorsports. A mere two months after that decision, Montez Stewart was sitting on the starting grid at Daytona—the first AMA race of the season—on a Yamaha R6. The bike was bathed in Carolina Blue (the official color of MJ's alma mater, the North Carolina Tar Heels), and Stewart's leathers matched the bike's distinctive livery. Clad with the "Jumpman" logo (the silhouette of Michael Jordan midair, his legs splayed apart while palming a basketball), Stewart and his bikes were highly visible as he competed in the 600-cc Supersport and 1,000-cc Superstock series. Jordan's presence at events was sensational, and in spite of the team's growing pains, crowds were electrified. Later in the season, General Manager Ken Abbott introduced Jordan to Jason Pridmore, whom Jordan later assisted after the No Limits racing team experienced financial difficulties. Pridmore, who was a champion in the 2003 FIM World Endurance, 2002 AMA Formula Extreme 1000cc, and 1997 AMA 750 Superstock competitions, affixed a Jumpman logo onto his Suzuki as a gesture of gratitude.

This whistle incorporates several symbols. Its primary shape comes from the letters CPH, which refer to Jordan's inspirational high school basketball coach, Clifton Pop Herring. The word "Every" represents Jordan's commitment to whole-heartedly pursue every competition he undertakes. The icon next to "Every" incorporates numerous aspects of symbology, including the three dots (which represent the beginning, middle, and end), and the circle (which represents the unbroken circle of continuousness).

44+1 refers to how Jordan chose his No. 45 NBA designation following a brief stint in baseball. Jordan's hero and inventor of the alley-oop, David Thompson, was No. 44; by taking No. 45, he was simply "adding himself," plus 1, to his hero.

A reference to Larry Bird, the rival and peer who, along with David Thompson and Julius Irving, Jordan counts among his top three influences.

This is a 1976 Chevrolet Monte Carlo, Jordan's first car. His silhouette is visible in the back seat and refers to his being suspended in 10th grade for mischievous behavior before he took up basketball the following year.

A combination of several symbols: the word "Pops" spells out the shape of the toolbox, representing Michael Jordan's father, who was a "fix-it" man. 178 is the highest known speed that Jordan has reached on a motorcycle on the street; the velocity was achieved on his Ducati 998.

In honor of Tinker Hatfield, who designed Air Jordans III through XV; the "3-15" refers those shoes. He was also a mentor and special consultant on Air Jordans XVI through XIX.

In honor of Dean Smith, head coach for the University of North Carolina Tarheels.

69 was Jordan's career high for points in a game, which he scored against Cleveland in March 1990.

Designed by Mark Smith, this "23" was the first iteration of Jordan's Chicago Bulls number. Subsequent versions appearing on leathers, helmets, and motorcycles incorporated his tribal-inspired patterns.

This home plate symbol incorporates some of Jordan's key baseball stats from his time spent playing with the Birmingham Barons: 3 home runs, 51 RBIs, and 30 stolen bases.

These patterns recall the number 6, the amount of NBA championships Michael Jordan won.

Maori tattoos were earned through courageous deeds, and this image of Jordan's heavily tattooed face designed by Mark Smith suggests that he is a warrior of great power.

Michael Jordan's friends refer to him as "Black Cat," and this feline silhouette recalls his graceful on-court style.

The product of a synthesis of African-American and popular culture, this design detail was taken from the outsole of the Air Jordan VII shoe.

The Jumpman logo, the mark of the Jordan brand, first appeared on the Air Jordan III.

A close-up detail from the synthetic elephant print of the Air Jordan III.

Though dice may appear to suggest Jordan's fondness for gambling, they actually refer to his love of risk versus reward during competition.

Commemorates the Air Jordan XX and the 20th anniversary of the brand franchise.

The shoebox refers to Jordan's tradition of wearing a brand-new pair of Air Jordans out of the box before each game.

Symbolizes the bus driver's hat, a golf game Jordan plays with friends in which the lowest scorer is forced to wear an embarrassing hat.

Six stars commemorate Michael Jordan's six NBA championships. 10. In honor of Tate Kuerbis, senior footwear designer for the Jordan brand and chief designer of the Air Jordan XVIII.

Despite a relatively well-funded privateer effort, Michael Jordan Motorsports had a steep learning curve during its debut year. For the 2005 season, Jordan introduced two more riders under his banner: Jason Pridmore and Steve Rapp. While struggling to adjust to the demands of his larger team, Jordan was also, in a sense, getting up to speed in a different way. "I feel like I am playing catch-up because I was away from it for so many years," he said. "I am a big, avid fan. It's in my blood right now." The challenge of producing a fresh design for the 2005 bikes also recalled a bigger issue for Jordan. Most AMA teams tend not to exert much effort on the appearance of their bikes and apparel, but while launching his team, Jordan's goals were not just to win but also to uphold his iconic legacy. Having established his global brand identity with the revolutionary line of Nike "Air Jordan" sneakers, Jordan knew very well the importance of forward-thinking style and distinctive appearance.

Flash back to 1985, when Michael Jordan viewed the first ever prototype for the Air Jordan I shoe. He had a difficult time wrapping his head around the then-radical design, which incorporated a red-on-black color scheme. He said he was afraid it would make him look like a "clown," but Nike designer Peter Moore was resolute. When Jordan wore the shoes on the court, he stood out so prominently against the monochromatic sea of sneakers that NBA commissioner David Stern fined him for his distracting footwear. Nike—sensing the potential for positive publicity—paid the fines for Jordan numerous times, and the consumer version of the controversial shoes became a huge seller, rewriting the unofficial rulebook of retail sneaker merchandising.

Twenty years later, Jordan's sophomore year of AMA racing presented him with a similar design challenge. He asked Mark Smith, a colleague of Tinker Hatfield (who was responsible for the design of 14 iterations of Air Jordan shoes) to create a race bike graphic incorporating yellow, black, and red. The finished product disconcerted Jordan. "The bike [looked] like somebody wrecked it and put it back together with what they could find," he would say in his book, *Driven from Within.* "I'm laughing now because I know the kind of response I'm going to get within the race community."

The motorcycle racing community is, in fact, a tightly knit sliver of society that has operated under its own rules for decades, but Jordan Motorsports provided exactly the sort of shakeup that can broaden a sport to a new crop of fans. The 2005 bike's design direction echoed the iconoclastic spirit of Air Jordan I—the shoe that shamelessly boasted the shock of the new—while incorporating design cues from the Air Jordan XX, which was released in 2005. The relationship was synergistic: echoing the shoe, the bike's tank and racer's left racing-suit arm are covered in iconographic symbology reflecting milestones, accomplishments, and references to Jordan's personal and professional life, while the shoe features textural treatments inspired by motorcycle tire tread and shifter toe pads. (The Air Jordan XX is not the first shoe to reference Jordan's love of fast machines; the VI was inspired by NASA's experimental X-15 aircraft, XIV alluded to his Ferrari 550M, and XVII incorporated detailing based on an Aston Martin.)

Michael Jordan's "Jumpman" logo merges his basketball history with his motorcycle racing endeavors.

Beneath the striking skin of Jason Pridmore's No. 43 GSX-R 1000 is an inline four-cylinder powerplant that produces over 180 horsepower at 13,500 rpm, propelling the 366-pound bike to a top speed of 195 miles per hour. Competing in the Superstock class for modified street bikes, Pridmore battled his way through the season until a potentially fatal crash forced him to sit out five events, leading new teammate Steve Rapp to stand in. By season's end, Rapp was able to secure a third-place position in the 2005 Superstock points championship. While Jordan Motorsports continued to battle the big boys in the 2006 season, it also took its signature a step further by integrating a gold metal theme with a glittery graphics treatment.

In 2006, Montez Stewart was replaced with Jake Holden, a promising young upstart who slowly marched toward the front of the field until he crashed at the Mid-Ohio season closer. Incorporating principles gleaned from his experiences in professional basketball, Jordan intends to continue his racing efforts in the hopes of eventually winning—something he became quite accustomed to during his reign in the NBA. He has imposed his singular style on AMA racing and injected a new level of interest in the sport, thanks to his larger-than-life personality. Regarding new endeavors, of which Michael Jordan has had a few, his maxim encapsulates the spirit of his venture: "I can accept failure, but I can't accept not trying."

Pridmore's 2005 Jordan Suzukis await practice at Daytona Speedway. *Brian J. Nelson*

20

MIKE HAILWOOD'S

DUCATI COMEBACK BIKES

A Hero's Returns to the Isle of Man

Mike Hailwood's tremendous motorcycle racing achievements unfolded into a foray in Formula 1 automobile racing and a retirement due to injuries sustained from an accident at the German GP. And so it was with tremendous anticipation that, after an 11-year absence from motorcycle racing, he returned to the Isle of Man to compete on a Ducati in 1978.

The breadth of Hailwood's career reveals the significance of his decision. At the age of 21, he competed for Honda during its infancy and won a 250-cc world championship, making him the youngest world champion and setting a record that would stand for 23 years. In 1962, he signed with MV Agusta and became the first rider to win four consecutive 500-cc world championships. Hailwood's racing career would earn him an astounding 76 Grand Prix victories and nine world championships; it was no wonder he earned the nickname "Mike the Bike."

Opposite: Mike Hailwood accelerating out of Quarter Bridge on his way to victory in the 1978 Formula One TT. The win came after an 11-year absence from the sport. *Mick Woollett*

The desmodromic valve operation featured in Hailwood's 1979 bike is still incorporated into modern Ducatis.

His 1978 comeback would prove doubly dramatic because of its location. Throughout the course of his career, Mike Hailwood's name had been synonymous with the Isle of Man TT race, which he dominated with a total of 14 wins. The course also served as a backdrop for one of his most notorious victories: the 1967 vanquishing of longtime rival Giacomo Agostini. Following that monumental win, Hailwood found it an appropriate time to retire from motorcycle racing. Eleven years later, he returned—with great fanfare and high expectations—to compete in the 1978 Isle of Man TT, and he emerged triumphant on an 883-cc Ducati V-twin before the largest crowd ever assembled at the fabled course.

The 1978 victory was stunning; at the age of 38, Hailwood had defied conventional wisdom, beating competitors who were in their prime. High on his success and choosing to further push the odds, he returned the following year in hopes of a final fling—one last victory before retreating back into retirement. During the requisite testing in Italy two weeks before practice, Hailwood was to train on one of the two bikes built by NCR for the Ducati factory. In spite of clear instructions, one of the mechanics assembled the gear shifter backward on the Ducati 950 F1. While traveling down pit lane, Hailwood shifted into what he thought was second gear but was in fact first, sending him flying off the bike and into the Armco railing, which broke several of his ribs. The bike was a total loss, and Hailwood was left with no backup for the main event.

Further complicating his effort was Ducati's sudden refusal to insure the remaining bike, most likely because of the testing incident. Seeking to mediate a middle ground between the racing legend and the Italian manufacturer, Steve Wynne of Sport Motor Cycles Ltd. bought the bike from Ducati under the agreement that he would take responsibility for any accident or claim, while also agreeing to sell the bike back to Ducati in case of victory—a contract he would later call "a classic case of heads they win, tails I lose."

In addition to his injuries and the lack of practice, Hailwood had even more odds stacked against him. The 950 F1's engine produced 15 less horsepower than his winning 1978 bike, and it handled, in the words of Wynne, like "an uncontrollable pig." There was limited sorting done to the chassis during a sole day of testing at Oulton Park, but last-ditch efforts to make the machine more competitive were desperate, at best. A sister bike was obtained from which to cannibalize parts, but they didn't fit, so metal chairs were swiped from a hotel and their legs were sawed off, providing makeshift structural reinforcements that were incorporated into the bike's frame. Faced with a poor performer in a field of more powerful and agile bikes, Hailwood nonetheless fought hard and battled to finish the race. In spite of the bike's battery falling off on the last lap (due to a faulty carrier), he scrambled to reinstall it and cross the finish line. Mike Hailwood's 1979 comeback attempt resulted in fifth place, a position that was better than almost any other living rider could have achieved under those dire circumstances,

Right: Hailwood's 1979 Ducati 950 F1 appears to wear Ducati colors, but the red, white, and green scheme was actually inspired by Castrol oil, one of the bike's sponsors.

Below: The Ducati's heavy clutch action required two levers to be welded together for greater leverage.

but a standing that nonetheless fell short of the performance he was hoping for.

Hailwood rode the bike once more during a demonstration lap of TT week in 1980. According to Barber Vintage Motorsports Museum restorer Joe Bruton, it was the last bike he rode before his death in a tragic automobile accident the following year, which also claimed the life of his nine-year-old daughter.

Prior to its purchase by Alabama collector George Barber, Mike Hailwood's 1979 Ducati 950 F1 underwent chassis modifications by Ron Williams, chief suspension engineer for Honda Britain and tuner for racers including Joey Dunlop. Since Hailwood's final performance at the Isle of Man, Williams added braces around the steering head and reinforced the bike's frame, while replacing the twin rear Marzocchi shocks with more progressive Konis.

Joe Bruton has ridden the bike and says, "It's very obvious when you're riding it that it'll produce power until it blows up." The combination of the engine's relatively low power output and its high-strung nature was probably one of several factors that prevented Hailwood from emerging victorious in 1979.

In spite of the Ducati's inability to produce a finish that reflected Hailwood's uncommon skill, his final competition at the Isle of Man confirmed the widely held belief that the only thing more impressive than his riding talent was his character. Mike Hailwood's attitude and ethics were summarized by the message he painted on the fairing of an early race bike: "For love of the sport." Former mechanic Nobby Clark described Hailwood's passion by saying, "Today, the riders will race if the money is right. Mike wasn't that way; he loved to race." In a gesture that many considered to be an act of heroism consistent with his personality, during a Formula 1 Grand Prix race at the Nürburgring, Hailwood stopped midcourse to rescue fellow racer Clay Regazzoni, who was trapped in his burning car.

And thus it was the spirit of Hailwood's swan song, not his final standing in the race, that eventually led Ducati to produce a replica bike inspired by his infamous return to the Isle of Man. Despite the circumstances that dogged the 1979 bike, the replica recalls the grace, composure, and fighting spirit of Mike Hailwood the racing hero, and a legacy that will outlast the limitations of his last race machine.

21

MARTY DICKERSON'S

BLUE BIKE

Bonneville's Irresistible Allure

The "salt bug"—as described by those smitten by it—refers to the alluring expanse of seemingly endless salt flats and its implicit promise of speed. It strikes free-spirited souls in search of ultimate velocity, and during his first trip to Bonneville in 1950, Marty Dickerson fell under its spell.

An avid street racer, Dickerson owned two Harleys before falling for the more lightweight and powerful 1946 Triumph Tiger 100. Dedication to the street racing scene meant countless hours fraternizing at garages, and while hanging out at an Indian shop, Dickerson became a frequent audience for a Scotsman who raved incessantly about Vincent motorcycles. According to the man's claims, Vincents were capable of dropping a gear and leaving a black stretch of rubber, yet could also float over railroad crossings like a featherbed. Curious about this "other" British motorcycle, Dickerson finally visited the Burbank, California, showroom of Vincent salesman Vince "Mickey" Martin, and his first impression

Opposite: Marty Dickerson's *Blue Bike*, which is now owned by Herb Harris.

Marty Dickerson looks down the course as he prepares for a salt flat run. The first clock is about 2 miles away. *Herb Harris*

was strong: "God those things were ugly," Dickerson recalls, "but I was visualizing power, and they definitely looked like they were fast."

Fast they were, but Vincents were also expensive. Dickerson, who wanted an upgrade, tried to strike a deal with Martin but couldn't negotiate a high enough value for his chromed-and-customized Triumph. Nonetheless, Vincents continued to be a source of fascination for Dickerson, and during one of his many Saturday afternoons spent talking shop with Martin, he discovered that the talkative Scotsman had to give up his bike. Dickerson would take $800 for his Triumph, which went to the Scotsman, and he financed the difference for a brand-new 1948 Series "B" Rapide—sequence No. 727, one of the first imported to the United States.

Dickerson adored his Rapide—which would come to be called the *Blue Bike*—but he had difficulty keeping up with payments. Martin, hoping to create a win-win solution for Dickerson's financial problems, suggested a novel idea: tour the Southwest with the bike and show off its speed in order to build opportunities to establish new Vincent dealerships. Dickerson, who was willing to try anything to keep the Vincent, attached soft bags to the *Blue Bike* and set out across America on what was essentially a goodwill drag racing and public relations tour. "Every town I went to," he recalls, "I had to race the fastest thing around. I beat everybody; I even beat six cops riding 80-cubic-inch Indian Black Hawk Chiefs in Arlington, Texas. There was no contest," he adds, "but I came back a week later, and they said that because they were working for the city, they had to buy American products." His tour continued through Oklahoma and back through New Mexico, and while he gathered crowds and proved his (and his bike's) prowess through drag races, the trip never led to a sale or dealership franchise. In Dickerson's absence, Martin graciously covered his bike payments.

The *Blue Bike* saw more usage back in Los Angeles, and regular drag races kept Dickerson's reaction time sharp and his riding skills honed. After picking up a copy of *Life* magazine that featured the famous photograph of Rollie Free's prone, record-breaking ride on the *John Edgar Lightning*, Dickerson became intrigued enough to ride the *Blue Bike* up to Bonneville in 1950, a trip that pushed its odometer to the 28,000-mile mark. Free, who suffered a high-speed crash on the flats but emerged unscathed, needed an extra hand removing the damaged fairing from his motorcycle. Dickerson assisted, then watched Free break his own world record with a 156.58-mile-per-hour run, *sans* fairing. The 1950 trip to Bonneville galvanized Dickerson's fascination; he vowed to convert his bike to speed-trial specifications, and his ride from Utah back to Los Angeles would be the last time his blue Rapide saw civilian use.

Driving his mother's car for daily transportation, Dickerson proceeded to modify his *Blue Bike* in the hope of competing the following year at Bonneville. He met Phil Vincent at Martin's shop and inquired into the cost of Lightning cams and pipes. "Son," Vincent said to the aspiring racer, "speed is expensive." Evidently, however, Martin had spoken well of Dickerson, and several weeks later, in early 1951, Dickerson received a long box in the mail containing Lightning camshafts, drive chain pipes, and an encouraging note from Vincent. Dickerson had no dynamometer with

which to calibrate his engine, so he adhered strictly to Vincent specifications. He added Black Shadow carbs and stuck to the factory specs, saying, "I used Bonneville—the big white dyno, as they call it—as my dyno."

Bonneville's Class C rules were relatively simple: bikes needed a workable kick-starter, a seat, handlebars with their original mounts, and an engine with stock bore and stroke running on pump gas using a compression ratio no higher than 8:1. In 1951, the year following his first Bonneville visit, he ran his *Blue Bike*—now modified with clever rule-abiding tricks like a small pad in place of a seat and upside-down handlebars—and established the 1,000-cc Class C record with a two-way average of 129 miles per hour. Following his Bonneville debut, Dickerson added brakes to his Vincent and road raced it. His speed record was broken in 1952 by Sam Parriott on an Ariel Square Four, and 1953 saw an impressive rebuttal from Dickerson: he broke the 150-mile-per-hour barrier on one run and clocked an average two-way speed of 147 miles per hour, a new record that would stand for an amazing 20 years before being broken by a Yoshimura Kawasaki Z1 in 1973.

Dickerson's presence at Bonneville introduced him to all the players—both famous and obscure—in the land speed scene. In 1955, he met Joe Simpson, who had broken Rollie Free's record in 1953 only to have Free take it back by a few hundredths of a second a few weeks later. Simpson was having mechanical problems with his supercharged Vincent Black Lightning, and Dickerson's expertise impressed him so much that he eventually asked Dickerson to run it. Marty pulled a two-way average of 177 miles per hour, allowing him to take the nonstreamlined land-speed record from BMW.

The *Blue Bike*'s workable kick-starter, along with other key features such as stock bore and stroke, enabled it to compete in Bonneville's Class C division.

In 1956, Dickerson met New Zealander and land-speed enthusiast Burt Munro, who was visiting Bonneville for the first time. Munro approached Dickerson because he was wearing a Vincent T-shirt, and after hitting it off, Munro hitched a ride with him back to Los Angeles, forging a friendship that would last several decades.

Dickerson, who had set up a shop in Hawthorne and taken over Martin's business, eventually fell on hard times. "Nineteen fifty-seven was really slow," he remembers. "We had a big recession, and once I only took in 54 cents in two weeks." He worked reduced hours and joined a government think tank in Santa Barbara in order to pay the bills. Dickerson maintained his passion throughout the 1960s by teaching motorcycle maintenance at a vocational school and returned to the salt flats yearly. Because the new higher-compression-ratio limit favored Japanese bikes such as the Yoshimura Kawasaki, his comeback attempts with the *Blue Bike* were not as successful as he had hoped. Dickerson squeezed as much power out of the British engine as he could muster, but the combination of the 4,000-foot altitude and a new rule requiring 110 octane fuel worked against his bike's unsophisticated technology. However, at the age of 70, Dickerson returned to Bonneville in 1996 and succeeded in taking home a record in the Vintage class.

The *Blue Bike*'s cleverly mounted upside-down handlebars stayed within Class C regulations, while facilitating a wind-cheating lower profile.

This aftermarket exhaust hugs the Vincent's body more closely than stock pipes.

After almost 50 years of improvements to his *Blue Bike*, Dickerson took collector Herb Harris up on an offer to sell the motorcycle. In its current state, the *Blue Bike* reflects the accumulation of decades of evolution, including heads ported and polished by master tuner Jerry Branch, sodium-filled valves sourced from a Chrysler Hemi V-8, and a low-profile tank with 1 inch shaved off the bottom for improved aerodynamics. In spite of its countless runs on the corrosive salt flats, the bike's bodywork remains in remarkably good shape.

The *Blue Bike* went through countless iterations at the hands of Marty Dickerson, and though he still enjoys maintaining and riding other marques, he will always be intimately associated with the bike that took him to Bonneville for the first time in 1950. At his 80th birthday party in 2006, a series of three photographs was on display. The shots, which were taken in 1953, 1975, and 1996, feature Dickerson standing behind his *Blue Bike* on the flats. A banner above reads, "Happy 80th Birthday Marty. Some Things Never Change!!! (But People Do)." Herb Harris encapsulates the significance of the *Blue Bike* as "more than a motorcycle. This was his companion. Marty's had three wives but only one Vincent twin," he adds. "She never did him wrong."

Marty Dickerson's relationship with his *Blue Bike* spanned almost 50 years. *Herb Harris*

22

BURT MUNRO'S

MUNRO SPECIAL

The World's Fastest Indian

Everyone remembers the first time they fell in love. For Herbert James Munro, that moment came in 1920 when he laid eyes on a brand-new Indian Scout parked at a garage in Invercargill, New Zealand. Elegant bodywork surrounded the bike's cast-alloy V-twin engine, and the 21-year-old motorcycle enthusiast knew he had to have one. Munro used his life's savings to buy the Indian for £140 from friend and dealer Archie Prentice, and a month later, he received delivery of his dream bike.

He was forced to sell the Indian when he got married and moved to Australia for work. The red Indian was not easily forgotten, and upon his return to his native New Zealand in 1929, he tracked down the bike's second owner, only to discover that he had already resold it to someone else. Upon finally locating the bike, Munro talked him into selling back the dilapidated motorcycle for £1.

Opposite and above: Push-starting the *Munro Special* required the efforts of several men, which often included Rollie Free and Marty Dickerson. *Marty Dickerson collection*

The *Munro Special* was usually towed to the salt flats on a rickety trailer. *Marty Dickerson collection*

Newly reunited, Munro joined the Southland Motorcycle Club and subjugated his Indian to dramatic modifications in order to keep it competitive. He sought to improve the Indian's side-valve engine by hand-filing its cam profiles and raising its compression level. The more aggressive cams strained the valve action, which required stiffer springs—all of which created an ongoing struggle to find the subtle middle ground between valve float and valve bounce. In the process, the engine consumed many a valve, and by pulling replacements from cars and sculpting them down to size on a lathe, Munro sunk deeper into what would become a lifelong obsession.

Recognizing the dynamically interrelated nature of engine components, Munro would improve one part, which in turn would cause another part to fail, forcing him to continually upgrade the weakest link. Like an alchemist, he experimented with metal formulations by melting down varying proportions of automobile pistons on the 2-gallon furnace in his workshop. As he continued to tweak his Indian's powerplant, it began to have very little resemblance to the original 1920 technology that was fading into obsolescence.

Munro operated almost entirely on intuition, imagining the inner workings of his engine and modifying its configuration accordingly. After visualizing the combustion process inside the cylinders, for instance, he repositioned the spark plugs so they burned more efficiently. The bike was tested on the beach or at Ryal Bush Straight, a long stretch of highway not far from the work shed where he lived, and in between races and speed trials he relentlessly improved what would become

The *Munro Special* is seen here with a triple tail, one of numerous configurations that Munro experimented with. *Marty Dickerson collection*

The curvaceous shape of Munro's streamliner was inspired by goldfish. *Marty Dickerson collection*

known as the *Munro Special*. Carbs got enlarged and then replaced, the wheelbase grew longer and rear sets were installed (allowing him to stretch his legs back), and the handlebars were dropped for further aerodynamic streamlining.

By 1935, Munro was producing great leaps in his engine's performance, and he continued his quest for power while stubbornly refusing to beef up the bike's meager brakes. At a speed trial in 1940 he hit 120.8 miles per hour, which made him the fastest man in New Zealand—a speed record that held for almost 12 years.

Unsatisfied with a mere notation in the record books, Munro continued to equip his bike to go even faster. Realizing that he had approached the performance limits of a 600-cc engine, he bored out the cylinders to 633 cc. The next limitation was the engine's side-valve configuration, and he finally leapfrogged it by building a double-overhead-cam assembly. At a speed trial in 1951, Munro was timed at 133.33 miles per hour, but as much as his Indian was capable of record-breaking performance, it was also capable of breaking. Recognizing his engine's high failure rate, he sought to increase both reliability and performance, so he boosted displacement again to 738 cc. After unearthing buried city pipes, he bored them into what would become incredibly durable cylinders. He found Caterpillar tractor axles to be extremely strong and fashioned sturdy connecting rods from them. Die-cast steel pistons rounded out his newly reinforced powerplant, and

Burt Munro and his homegrown streamliner became hugely popular at Bonneville. *Marty Dickerson collection*

though a 1,000-cc streamlined Vincent Rapide broke his record in 1952, Munro took the New Zealand Beach Open Capacity Flying Half Mile record in 1953.

Perhaps inspired by the streamlined Vincent that finally broke his record, or the aluminum-shelled NSU streamliner that captured his imagination while visiting the Isle of Man TT, Munro felt that his bike needed to take yet another quantum leap toward achieving greater velocities. The inevitable answer was an aerodynamic one: Munro would streamline his Indian.

The curves of his streamliner were inspired by the slippery shape of goldfish, and in order to properly research the design, he planned a trip to the mecca of flat-out speed, Utah's Bonneville Salt Flats. The 1956 journey would be formative; he would meet Rollie Free, who had become famous from his record-breaking, bathing suit–clad ride, and Marty Dickerson, who, like Munro, nurtured a lifelong relationship with one bike. In fact, after the monumental experience of watching a variety of cars, motorcycles, and purpose-built one-offs compete for speed on the flats, Munro hitched a ride to Los Angeles in the back of Dickerson's pickup truck. He was indoctrinated into Dickerson's circle of friends, and the experience cemented his fascination with America. It would be the first of 14 visits to the United States.

After being awarded money pooled from the crowd, Burt Munro celebrates with an enthusiastic embrace.

The *Munro Special* is currently owned by the Hensley family.

While he continued to set records in his homeland, Munro's heart remained at the salt flats. Returning in 1957, he bought a decrepit Plymouth coupe for $28 and drove it to the flats, where he met Stirling Moss, John Vesco, and Bill Bagnall, the *Motorcyclist* editor who would write a profile about the ambitious New Zealander. The story would misspell Bert's name as Burt, but Munro was so endeared by the inadvertent Americanization that he adopted it as his written moniker.

When he finally brought the *Munro Special* to the United States in 1962, he found an oil-thirsty 1940 Nash, purchased it for $65, and drove from Long Beach to Seattle to pick up his bike. U.S. customs demanded a $10,000 bond, and after some tense moments, Munro persuaded an official to use a loophole to allow the bike in without charge. He then proceeded to Wendover, a small town adjacent to the flats.

At the salt flats, amid the seasoned speed seekers, Munro stood out in his dress pants and antiquated leather jacket. His Indian's hand-shaved tires had a section that was cut down too far, and, noticing a piece of exposed cord, Rollie Free advised Munro to make sure the bald spot was on the ground when the bike underwent inspection.

After passing its tech inspection, speed trial manager Earl Flanders insisted that the bike perform a trial run on the flats before officially competing. Followed by officials in a chase vehicle, the Indian accelerated out of their sight at 90 miles per hour, and by about 120 miles per hour developed a serious wobble, which would remain Munro's little secret until he shared it later with Free and Dickerson. In spite of the vibration problem, Munro started his timed run with a push from his friends and slipped the clutch until about 50 miles per hour, holding first until he shifted into second gear at around 90 miles per hour. The bike wobbled heavily between 100 and 140 miles per hour—at which point he shifted into third gear—and as he powered his way into top gear, he struggled to maintain control of the bike as his front tire rubbed against the leaf spring suspension, spewing hot rubber in his face.

The return run was equally dramatic, but Munro was intent on making good use of his inaugural trip to Bonneville. His leg, which lay perilously close to the Indian's scalding exhaust pipe, began to burn from the flimsily shielded metal. He hit top speed during the run, but shortly thereafter ran out of gas and wandered off course, only to be chased down by the exasperated, but relieved, Free and Dickerson. Flanders informed Munro that he was a new national record holder with his average speed of 178.971 miles per hour. Still unsatisfied, Munro spent 48 hours repairing the 850-cc engine's bent valves and melted piston, only to suffer more engine problems and a clutch malfunction that would injure his leg and ruin his chances of breaking the record the second time around.

Munro returned to New Zealand and pursued his compulsion by feverishly developing new ways to speed up and stabilize the Indian. He returned to Bonneville in 1963 and managed a run of

Either side of the *Munro Special*'s bodywork can be removed, revealing the structure beneath.

183.667 miles per hour, the fastest speed of the week for any competitor, but engine and high-speed stability issues still dogged him. In order to aid stability, a pilot urged him to remove the lead weight from the rear of the body and bias more weight toward the front. Munro would later express his realization in a letter: "The cure [to wobbling] is to sit-up [*sic*] and let the body strike the air. This shifts the center of pressure back behind [the] center of gravity. I learned this the hard way."

Munro made an arrangement to leave his streamliner at the San Gabriel, California, shop of Indian specialist Sam Pierce while he took the engine back to New Zealand to finesse it. Munro's Bonneville visits were almost becoming routine; again and again he would return to the flats, blow out engines, and frantically work around the clock to get back on the salt. He experimented by sourcing connecting rods from DC6 propellers, grafting airplane winglets onto the rear tail, lowering the nose, and cutting an 8-inch inlet hole that channeled air to exhaust ports in the rear of the streamliner. The majority of his efforts focused on engine improvements, and toward the end of Munro's excursions to Bonneville, he intensified his efforts to hit the mystical 200-mile-per-hour barrier. In its final configuration, the Munro Scout boasted a 985-cc engine capacity, and the cylinders were bored so close together that one of his repairs involved constructing thicker liners for the barrels. The V-twin powerplant pumped out well over six times more power than it did in 1920, and in 1967, he set a one-way record of 190.07 miles per hour and a new national record with an average speed of 183.586 miles per hour, earning him a Top Record Breaker trophy.

At the age of 71, Munro realized that his visit to Bonneville in June 1970 might be his last opportunity to break the 200-mile-per-hour barrier. At the flats, against the advice of Free and

Dickerson, friend Jim Enz and his wife offered to buy Munro 5 gallons of expensive Mickey Thompson-formulated nitromethane fuel. "Boy, was it the best piston burner!" Munro would later say. "I guess it had Nitro or TNT in it. Every run the pistons vaporized." Nitromethane, which burns considerably hotter than the methanol he had been using, requires a rich mixture in order to combust effectively and can effortlessly burn holes into pistons when the blend is off. Blowing out the engine during several runs, Munro frenetically replaced pistons and ran again, only to keep encountering the same problem. When he ran out of replacement pistons, he tried welding together the least damaged of his scrap pile but ran out of time.

Burt Munro passed away in 1978, and the *Munro Special*—which encapsulated over 50 years of continual development, rebuilding, and modification—was stored by the Pierce family until 1981. Having purchased it from Munro during the 1970s, Sam Pierce sold it to Gordy Clark. In the mid-1980s, Dean Hensley purchased the bike from Doug Clark, who had taken possession of it after it had been left in a state of neglect. Hensley and master restorer Steve Huntzinger undertook an ambitious and meticulous restoration that was completed in 1987. The bike is now owned by the Hensley family and is in the care of Tom Hensley.

The *Munro Special*, serial number 5OR627, is not only one of the earliest Indian Scouts built, it is also one of the most unique. Through the tenacity of one man, its fundamentally simple design became elaborated upon exponentially. This dialogue between Munro and his bike inspired the 2005 film *The World's Fastest Indian*, which stars Sir Anthony Hopkins as the velocity-obsessed New Zealander. Though the 1920 Indian Scout never permitted Munro to live his dream of joining the 200-mile-per-hour club, it enabled him to live a life of adventure, curiosity, and fulfillment that most only dream of.

Burt Munro incorporated a modified overhead valve assembly, which enabled quantum leaps in his bike's performance.

23

RENZO PASOLINI'S

HARLEY-DAVIDSON XR750

Italo-American Chemistry

Harley-Davidson, in a business move reflecting a prescient level of global awareness, ventured with Italian firm Aermacchi to develop small motorcycles in the 1960s. The alliance sought to capitalize on Aermacchi's expertise with compact two- and four-stroke bikes, a market Harley believed could lure a new generation of riders that would eventually graduate to its bigger, more expensive motorcycles.

Concurrent with the cross-cultural merger was the rise of a popular Italian road racer by the name of Renzo Pasolini. Aggressive, talented, and passionate, Pasolini had a background in motocross and began road racing for Aermacchi in 1964. He valiantly competed against multicylinder bikes on an Aermacchi single and established his reputation as a fighter by finishing third in 1966's 350-cc Grand Prix, behind Mike Hailwood and Giacomo Agostini. Riding for Benelli in 1968, he won the 250-cc

Opposite: Pasolini's Harley-Davidson was originally built for Bart Markel to ride in AMA dirt track events and was later converted to road racing spec.

Top: Pasolini riding at Ontario, California, in 1972. *Dan Mahony*
Above: Dual Mikuni carbs feed the 45-degree V-twin powerplant, which is capable of sending the Harley to a top speed of 160 miles per hour.

and 350-cc Italian National championships and finished second behind Agostini in the 350-cc world championship.

His fierce rivalry with Agostini would continue, but Ago's superior MV Agustas often relegated Pasolini to the reluctant role of underdog, forcing him into second place eight times in the 1968 season. Nevertheless, the competition bred passionate race fans, and the two became national heroes in their native Italy while battling the likes of Phil Read, Jarno Saarinen, Barry Sheene, and Kel Carruthers.

Meanwhile, Harley's involvement with the Italian manufacturer was becoming more intense, and by the late 1960s, almost half of all Harleys sold were sourced from Aermacchi. In 1971, Pasolini's return to Aermacchi would put him in the seat of a Harley. That season, during a rider swap program, Pasolini rode the last of the iron-barreled iterations of the XR750 in Ontario, California, and finished in fourth position—the highest of all Harley riders—edging out Mert Lawwill, Mark Brelsford, and Cal Rayborn, who crashed.

Taking his momentum into the 1972 250-cc Grand Prix season under the Aermacchi banner, Pasolini narrowly missed winning the championship by only one point, behind Jarno Saarinen, and landed behind Saarinen and Agostini in the 350-cc class. While in the States, he raced on a Harley-Davidson XR750 that was originally built for Bart Markel for competition in AMA dirt track events. Converted to road racing specs by top-dog AMA tuner Bill Werner, the dual-carbureted air-cooled 750-cc V-twin produced approximately 90 horsepower, weighed 320 pounds, and was capable of 160 miles per hour; the juxtaposition of big, brawny American power with an Italian rider was a spectacular sight, and Harley-Davidson's presence in Europe won crowds over and created a new fan base.

But soon after his promising season, tragedy would strike the 34-year-old racer. At Monza on May 20, 1973, Pasolini was riding for Aermacchi in the 250-cc GP race when he entered Monza's La Curva Grande. Losing control of his bike, Pasolini and Jarno Saarinen (who was just behind him on a Yamaha) were killed instantly in an accident that also involved six other riders. Though rumors abound that the collision was caused by an engine seizure on Pasolini's bike, the prevailing theory is that an oil spill from the previous 350-cc race led to the fatal loss of control.

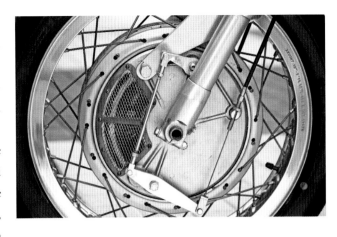

Front four-shoe Fontana drum brakes and a rear single-disc system were responsible for stopping the Harley.

Harley-Davidson's rebadged Aermacchi bikes would go on to win three consecutive years of 250-cc Roadracing World Championships between 1974 and 1976, as well as the 350-cc World Championship in 1976.

Pasolini's passing sent shockwaves through the GP community, hitting rival Giacamo Agostini particularly hard. The Harley-Davidson XR750 ridden by Renzo Pasolini in 1972 represents the union of an iconic American brand and a charismatic Italian racer, whose willful spirit was memorialized 13 years after his death with Ducati's release of the Paso, a Massimo Tamburini–designed tribute bike in honor of Pasolini.

During a rider swap, Italian Renzo Pasolini made this 1972 XR750 the highest-finishing Harley at Ontario Speedway in California. *Dave Friedman photo/Don Emde collection*

PHIL READ'S
MV AGUSTA GP BIKES

MV's Last Hurrah

Grand Prix motorcycle racing is a delicate microcosm where fortunes can shift rapidly. While competing technology, rider allegiances, and luck can coalesce to edge a marque from its top spot, during the early 1970s, MV Agusta's GP racing program faced even larger threats. Count Domenico Agusta, who led the company to an astounding 13 consecutive 500-cc world championships, established racing supremacy through deep-pocketed spending, ongoing technological advances, and alliances with the world's greatest riders. But his sudden death in 1971 robbed the company of its most ardent supporter and created a domino effect threatening to upset MV's dominance.

Seven years prior to Agusta's death, in the midst of MV Agusta's GP heyday, British racer Phil Read earned Yamaha its first world title with a 250-cc crown. Throughout the 1960s, he battled archrival Mike Hailwood, and in 1968, Yamaha ordered him to win only the 125-cc title.

Oppostite: Phil Read braking for the La Source hairpin at Spa on the 500-cc GP bike. *Mick Woollett*

Read at the Belgian
Grand Prix's La Source
hairpin in 1973.
Mick Woollett

After a disagreement with teammate Bill Ivy, he decided otherwise: "I thought I would try to win both," he says, "and I did." Exiled from Yamaha for his heedlessness in winning both 125-cc and 250-cc championships, Read returned to the scene in 1971 as a privateer and, capitalizing on his engineering experience, proceeded to win his fifth world championship without any factory support. Reinforcing his hotshot image, Read broke Giacamo Agostini's 500-cc lap record during a one-off ride at Silverstone in 1972. MV Agusta, eager to keep its fire stoked, hired Read for the upcoming GP season to race its 500-cc bike alongside Agostini.

By 1973, the stakes were getting high at the Italian manufacturer, though its incredible track record might have impeded a reality check. "Because MV had been winning so easily for so long," explains Read, "what they were up against with two-strokes like Suzuki and Yamaha didn't really sink in." Phil Read was ready to uphold MV's legacy, and aware of relatively new technology that could be sourced from America, he arranged for disc brakes and lightweight magnesium wheels to be shipped to Europe and implemented on his bike. Skeptical MV Agusta company officials reluctantly incorporated the components, though quicker lap times changed their minds. After the first few races of the season, Read recalls them saying, "Phil, can you please get us some more?"

Read racing in 1973.
Don Emde collection

Phil Read racing a 500-cc MV Agusta at Mallory on June 9, 1974, on his way to delivering the manufacturer's final 500-cc world championship. *Mortons*

As the season progressed, the chemistry of bike, rider, and team effort was proving effective. The 500-cc bike was particularly well suited to the Spa-Francorchamps circuit, and Read described the experience of riding it there: "The sound of the MV would reverberate between the hills as it accelerated away from La Source, passed the pits, up and through Eau Rouge, and away into the country." Phil Read and his potent bike would push the fabled Italian marque to victory in 1973, and the triumph put him at the top of his game while maintaining MV Agusta's reputation as a formidable force in GP racing.

Read would ride his 500-cc MV Agusta again the following year, but the battle was tougher. "By 1974," he explains, "the Japanese factory bikes were becoming faster on the corners as well as down the straights, and the MVs had never before needed to be ridden so hard and leaned over so far." Read eventually won the 1974 500-cc competition on his MV Agusta, which clinched his seventh and final Grand Prix Championship. That year would prove to be the manufacturer's last hurrah of Grand Prix racing, sealing a phenomenal 17 consecutive 500-cc and a record 37 total world championships. The next four-stroke 500-cc motorcycle to win a world championship would not come for another 28 years, during the 2002 Moto GP season.

The acme of MV Agusta's GP racing endeavors was captured in the 500-cc bikes that Phil Read took to victory in 1973 and 1974, concluding the manufacturer's sweeping preeminence in the sport. Since its final Grand Prix victory in 1974, MV Agusta has experienced waves of financial struggle, including several years of bankruptcy. Though Phil Read's 1973 and 1974 GP wins represent an era when the Italian bike builder proved it could dominate the world, it also provided a stark contrast to less successful times that have reinforced the unfortunate reality that sumptuously crafted, hand-built motorcycles are not guaranteed a place on Grand Prix podiums, let alone the modern marketplace. Looking back at his last two Grand Prix seasons for MV Agusta, Phil Read simply calls them "the experience of a lifetime."

Phil Read leading Barry Sheene at the Hutchinson 100 in 1975. That year, Read finished the Grand Prix season in second place for MV Agusta, in a battle that wasn't decided until the 10th and final round in Czechoslovakia. *Mortons*

25

ROBERT PIRSIG'S

HONDA CB77 SUPERHAWK

Inspiring Zen and the Art of Motorcycle Maintenance

On the surface, Robert M. Pirsig's *Zen and the Art of Motorcycle Maintenance* recalls a journey the author and his son, Chris, took in the summer of 1968 across the northwest United States on a 1964 Honda CB77 Superhawk. Pirsig, who studied Eastern philosophy in India during the 1950s, uses the novel to explain his worldview, a perspective that does not ascribe to Western concepts of wealth, materialism, and concern for outward appearance.

Despite the book's deceptively simple title, the storyline begins transcending the topics of motorcycle riding and maintenance, and grows into a challenging meditation on the relationships between science, philosophy, and humanism. Using the analogy of motorcycle maintenance, he clarifies his concept of quality: "Quality is the Buddha. Quality is scientific reality. Quality is the goal of Art. It remains to work these concepts

Opposite: Robert Pirsig and his son, Chris, rest on the Honda CB77 Superhawk at the Camp Buell State Historical Site in North Dakota. In *Zen and the Art of Motorcycle Maintenance*, Pirsig describes the landscape as "flattened into a Euclidian plane. Not a hill, not a bump anywhere."

Chris Pirsig and John and Sylvia Sutherland at a rest area off the Beartooth Pass Highway in Montana.

into a practical, down-to-earth context, and for this there is nothing more practical or down-to-earth than what I have been talking about all along—the repair of an old motorcycle."

By juxtaposing Eastern philosophy and Western logic, Pirsig connects two seemingly contradictory belief systems into one. In doing so, he dissolves the barriers between the man-made and the natural: "The Buddha, the Godhead, resides quite as comfortably in the circuits of a digital computer or the gears of a cycle transmission as he does at the top of a mountain or in the petals of a flower." He expounds upon the significance of quality, emphasizing the similarities between such seemingly disparate subjects as correct motorcycle maintenance and proper personal behavior.

While it dissects philosophy and reason, what distinguishes *Zen and the Art of Motorcycle Maintenance* is that it does so by celebrating the sensory experience of motorcycling—from the tactile pleasure of taking apart a bike, to the joy of riding across the country. On a bike, Pirsig explains, "You're completely in contact with it all. You're in the scene, not just watching it anymore, and the sense of presence is overwhelming. That concrete whizzing by five inches below your foot is the real thing, the same stuff you walk on, it's right there, so blurred you can't focus on it, yet you can put your foot down and touch it anytime, the whole thing, the whole experience, is never removed from immediate consciousness." Using his journey as a backdrop against which he delivers his meditations, the trip becomes a medium for countless thoughts and observations. Each destination and every interaction with his surroundings—both natural and human—becomes a tool with which his message can be more effectively conveyed.

Even Pirsig's choice of motorcycle speaks to his personal ideal of quality, which favors the elegance of function over the fleeting, and ultimately less satisfying, beauty of form. His friends, the Sutherlands, a married couple who accompany the Pirsigs for much of the journey on a 1968 BMW R60/2, hold completely different attitudes toward motorcycling and, subsequently, life. Because they have no interest in the inner workings of their BMW (even refusing to get their hands dirty in caring for their motorcycle), the author expresses a certain degree of disdain toward their point of view.

In Pirsig's mind, understanding the intimacies of how a mechanical object functions reflects an attitude of integrity; that level of caring is an indication of an innate appreciation of the thing he calls quality. The truth of the machine, and where it gets the rider—both physically and spiritually—is something that Pirsig relishes, particularly toward the end of the epic ride when he reflects upon his humble Honda, an object that has served him well: "Silver-grey and chrome and black and dusty. Dirt from Idaho and Montana and the Dakotas and Minnesota. From the ground up it looks very impressive. No frills. Everything with a purpose. I don't think I'll ever sell it . . . Quality. It's carried us so far without trouble."

Toward the end of the book, revelations about Pirsig's brilliant but troubled past—which includes mental illness, expulsion from school, and electroshock therapy—smolder alongside his continued attempts to connect with his emotionally distant son. The motorcycle ride, as it winds to an end, becomes a metaphor for the arc of human experience. Though he struggles with the demons of his past and the challenges of the present, the elemental simplicity of riding his Honda through rough weather and challenging circumstances provides Pirsig with a mechanism through which he can sort through life's complications and make sense of the world around him. "Trials never end, of course," he writes in the last lines of the book. "Unhappiness and misfortune are bound to occur as long as people live, but there is a feeling now, that was not here before, and is not just on the surface of things, but penetrates all the way through: We've won it. It's going to get better now. You can sort of tell these things."

Zen and the Art of Motorcycle Maintenance concludes on that optimistic note, but Robert Pirsig suffered a tragic postscript five years after the book was published. His son, Chris, while walking away from the San Francisco Zen Center, was mugged and stabbed to death. As Pirsig writes in the afterword of a later edition of the book, the loss of his son was countered with the unintended pregnancy of his second wife, creating a circular—and very Zen-like—series of events in his own life.

The BMW R60/2 ridden by the Sutherlands was sold before the book's publication to James Fellman, who sold it in 1977 to its current owner, Wisconsin architect Ollie Foran. Foran was unaware of the bike's provenance until the transaction was completed, and upon learning of the bike's origins felt honored and thrilled to own a piece of literary history. John Sutherland's signature and address appears on the bike's service book and Foran, incidentally, enjoys riding the BMW regularly.

The Honda CB77 that inspired *Zen and the Art of Motorcycle Maintenance* remains in the garage of Robert Pirsig. A request to interview Pirsig was declined, supporting his reputation as an enigmatic and reclusive personality.

Many bikes are legendary for their race successes or their associations with famous owners. But through a simple road trip, Robert Pirsig's Honda inspired one of the most widely read philosophy books of the twentieth century, while providing a poetic window into the world of motorcycling. The mystique of Pirsig's bike endures as a powerfully universal symbol for the journey of life. And in a way, that connection is wonderfully consistent with the nonmaterialistic, quality-based values so passionately advocated in *Zen and the Art of Motorcycle Maintenance*.

John Sutherland and Robert and Chris Pirsig at the Beartooth Pass rest area.

John Sutherland's BMW and Robert Pirsig's Honda are seen fully loaded up in this shot taken just south of Milnor, South Dakota. Chris excitedly holds binoculars, while John and Sylvia stand in the background.

26

STEVE MCQUEEN'S

GREAT ESCAPES

Riding with the King of Cool

"**I**'m not sure whether I'm an actor who races or a racer who acts," Steve McQueen once quipped. His delight in that ambiguity fueled his reputation as an incurable speed junky with a boyish obsession for collecting bikes and cars.

McQueen's tremendously successful acting career enabled hobbies like desert racing and aviation, and though he registered for races under the pseudonym of Harvey Mushman to avoid legal issues with film studios, the moniker also granted him the added benefit of anonymity. On screen, his fanaticism for fast bikes and cars seeped into his movie roles. The idea for the famous motorcycle jump in *The Great Escape*, for instance, came not from the mind of the film's director, but from McQueen himself. His facility with the Triumph (which was dressed up as a military-spec BMW) was so effortless that, although stuntman Bud Ekins was hired to perform the signature jump for insurance purposes, reverse angles of the German soldier aggressively tailing McQueen's character were also played by McQueen; the edited footage essentially depicts him chasing himself.

Opposite: Steve McQueen checks his watch during the 1964 International Six Days Trials.
Sean Kelly

McQueen rides his TR6SC Triumph through the streets of London prior to competing in the International Six Days Trials. *Sean Kelly*

Following his performance in *The Great Escape,* McQueen traveled to East Germany in 1964 to compete in the first organized American team effort at the International Six Days Trial (ISDT) competition. The event, which has been referred to as the "Olympics of Motorcycling," was a grueling test of man and machine—in McQueen's case, a Triumph TR6SC that was purchased by Bud Ekins from West Coast distributor Johnson Motors, Inc. Competition rules included marking major mechanical components with radium in order to ensure that nothing was tampered with; the only parts that could be changed during the event were chains, tires, headlight bulbs, and filter elements. Riders were permitted to make repairs to their bikes using their own tools. Led by Bud Ekins, who had participated in the ISDT four times before, the team of five American riders set out to East Germany to make their mark among the international crowd. Wearing Bell helmets personalized by Von Dutch, the U.S. team members rode hard until they hit a wall on day three. "After lunch on Wednesday, Steve crashed real bad," recalls Ekins. "He was physically OK, but the bike was bent so badly he couldn't ride it anymore. And within an hour, I broke my leg." He adds,

Steve McQueen's 1964 TR6SC ISDT Works Triumph was tracked down by Bud Ekins and Sean Kelly, and is currently owned by Kelly.

"But at noon on Wednesday, we were winning it—a bunch of amateurs!"

Following the event, McQueen's 1964 TR6SC ISDT Works Triumph was shipped back to California and ridden by Ekins in a Tijuana-to-La Paz record run. After McQueen sold the bike to Sacramento resident Frank Danielson, the new owner affixed a sidecar and raced it at the Baja 1000 three times, winning his class each time. Danielson, who still holds the Baja 1000 sidecar record, retired the bike in 1971 and sold it to Sean Kelly nearly 30 years later.

When Steve McQueen wasn't racing, he was acting, and following the success of *The Great Escape* he became one of Hollywood's most bankable stars. While negotiating for the lead role in *The Thomas Crown Affair*, he leveraged his participation so the filmmakers would incorporate a sequence in which he and Faye Dunaway romp on the beach in a high-performance dune buggy. The vehicle, which he described as being "set on a Volkswagen chassis... with a Corvair engine stuffed in the back," was co-designed by McQueen and produced about 230 horsepower while weighing only 1,000 pounds.

ISDT competitors were only allowed to work on their bikes using tools they carried with them.

High-performance machines continued to play an important role in his films, and the chase scene in 1968's *Bullitt*—widely considered to be one of the greatest of all time—features McQueen performing many of his own stunts, while Ekins stood in again for the riskiest maneuvers. Co-financing and appearing in *On Any Sunday,* Bruce Brown's ode to off-road motorcycle

Steve McQueen's 1926 Cleveland Fowler Four was photographed shortly before being auctioned from the late Otis Chandler's collection for $104,500.

racing, McQueen rode alongside pro racers Mert Lawwill and Malcolm Smith in the Lake Elsinore Grand Prix, breaking his foot but still managing an eighth-place finish. He would end up driving a Porsche 908 Spyder in the Sebring International Twelve Hour Endurance Race with his foot still broken, finishing first in class and second overall, ahead of none other than Mario Andretti. His speed pursuits merged again with the silver screen in 1971's *Le Mans*, a grittily minimalistic, documentary-style depiction of the infamous 24-hour endurance race, which further blurred the line between McQueen the actor and McQueen the racer.

McQueen amassed an eclectic collection of over 200 motorcycles, 55 cars, and five planes that tended toward the fast and the beautiful, though he also developed a penchant for the subtle and the anonymous. While living in an airplane hangar in Santa Paula during the renovation of his house, he and future wife Barbara Minty enjoyed cohabitating amid his growing collection. Friend Mario Iscovich described his living arrangement in the hangar as "being like a kid, being seven years old, and you have this incredible playroom with every conceivable toy." His vintage bike collection grew with the help of Bud Ekins and Stephen Wright, and McQueen placed wanted ads for motorcycles in *Hemmings Motor News*, personally answering each call from home.

Each mechanical toy was enjoyed for a different reason, and one bike he appreciated simply as an object of static beauty was

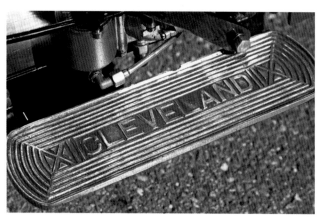

The Cleveland's detailed features include its floorboard.

his 1926 Cleveland Fowler Four. An extremely rare model, only a single-digit number of Fowler Fours exist, due to the inherently flawed design of its T-head engine, which prematurely halted production. McQueen loved finding a good bargain, and while inspecting the bike with Ekins and Wright, he saw that the Cleveland wouldn't start, so he negotiated a sale price of only $7,500. When Wright later inspected the bike, the mechanical trouble turned out to be minor, and he carefully restored it to its original glory. The bike's 600-cc side-valve four-cylinder engine sits exposed in its sparse frame, recalling a time when motorcycles still held vestigial design elements originating from bicycles. The Cleveland cost $375 when it was new and was sold at an auction of the late Otis Chandler in 2006 for $104,500.

McQueen had such an affinity for Indian motorcycles that he attempted, for some time, to own every model ever made—before realizing the impossibility of the task. He once drove 700 miles simply to see a rare 1915 Power Plus Indian with a sidecar. Because he sensed the owner's attachment to the bike, McQueen didn't bother making an offer. "I remember Steve's face as his eyes transfixed on it, you'd think he was looking at the Holy Grail," remembers Barbara McQueen in her memoir, *The Last Mile*.

The 1942 Indian Sport Scout on a bridge in Santa Paula, California, near the hangar where McQueen lived in the late 1970s.

The Scout features an elegantly curved shifter.

McQueen's personal 1942 Sport Scout got plenty of saddle time in the hills around Santa Paula. The Sport Scout model was relatively hard to find, since most Indians of the period were exported for World War II military forces. McQueen outfitted his with a Harley-Davidson seat because he felt its art deco intonations were better suited to the lines of the bike. While styled with grace, the Indian is difficult to ride gracefully. A lever on the left handgrip controls the mechanical timing advance, and stopping power comes predominantly from the rear brakes, which are operated by the right foot pedal. Because the so-called suicide clutch is worked by the left foot, when approaching a standstill the rider is required to deftly scrub off the last few miles per hour by using the right hand lever (which operates the weaker front brake) so the right foot can be placed on the ground when the bike comes to a stop. The Indian Sport Scout was once a part of the Otis Chandler collection and is now owned by Daniel Schoenewald.

By the late 1970s, McQueen developed a distinct interest in dropping off the radar. Until that time, his idea of avoiding attention was painting his voluptuous Jaguar XKSS a discreet shade of racing green. Later in life, he went for something a bit more rough-edged. In 1977, he purchased a run-down 1947 Indian Chief chopper that he would nickname *The Blob*, after the 1958 sci-fi film of the same name in which McQueen made his breakthrough performance. It became an escape vehicle he used when he needed to leave his movie star persona behind and become just another motorcyclist enjoying a ride. He injected a bit of forced authenticity into the bike by tying a sleeping bag to the sissy bar (purely for looks; he never intended to use it.) Chrome slip-on exhausts tips were wonderfully mismatched to the bike, as were the differently colored handgrips. The Indian's mangy appearance seemed to match McQueen's new look, which featured shoulder-length hair and an unkempt beard—allowing him to all but disappear on his sand-colored chopper. The bike was made slightly more reliable after maintenance by Indian expert Bob Stark and began to see more usage than many of McQueen's pristinely restored motorcycles. Steve McQueen's 1947 Indian Chief chopper is now owned by the National Motorcycle Museum in Anamosa, Iowa.

Fame and wealth enabled McQueen to build his expansive collection, but, toward the end of his life, it also allowed him to revert to the simple pleasures of wind in his hair and the unscripted possibilities of the winding road ahead. Sometimes fame opens doors and wealth facilitates the pursuit of indulgent hobbies, but when a passion runs bone deep, it does not necessarily need to be exercised on a rare, expensive machine. Steve McQueen was the type of enthusiast whose pulse quickened with just the right combination of bike and terrain; the sentiment was perhaps best captured when he said, "Every time I start thinkin' the world is all bad, then I start seein' some people out there havin' a good time on a motorcycle, and it makes me take another look."

Above: During the latter portion of his life, Steve McQueen's 1947 Indian Chief Chopper, dubbed *The Blob*, was the perfect complement to his unassuming new aesthetic. Note the mismatched handgrips.

Left: *The Blob* was well beyond being an old bike with patina; this close-up reveals the extent of its wear and tear.

TIMELINE

1920: Burt Munro falls in love with and purchases a brand new Indian Scout, which he later christens the *Munro Special.*

1935, May 13: Military and literary icon T. E. Lawrence collides with a bicyclist while riding his 1932 Brough Superior SS100. He dies six days later.

1944: Kenneth Howard, a.k.a. "Von Dutch," pinstripes his first motorcycle fuel tank at the age of 15.

1946: A 15-year-old James Dean is given his first real motorcycle, a 1947 CZ 125 cc.

1948, September 13: Rollie Free sheds his leathers and lays prone on the *John Edgar Lightning,* a modified Vincent Black Shadow, hitting a record 150.313 miles per hour at the Bonneville Salt Flats.

1950: Inspired by the famous photograph of Rollie Free riding the *John Edgar Lightning* in *Life* magazine, Marty Dickerson rides his *Blue Bike* to Bonneville for the first time.

1954: Dick Mann wins the amateur class at the Bay Meadows mile, launching a career that would last over 20 years and include two Grand National championships.

1955, September 30: James Dean dies at the age of 24 while driving his Porsche 550 Spyder to a race in Salinas, California.

1956: Elvis Aaron Presley and his 1956 Harley-Davidson Model K appear on the cover of the May 1956 issue of Harley's *Enthusiast* magazine, beginning a lifelong relationship with the brand.

1957: Leo Payne buys a new Harley Davidson Sportster from Mike Wilson's Cedar Rapids, Iowa, dealership. He later names it the *Turnip Eater.*

1961: Competing in the 250-cc class for Honda, Mike Hailwood becomes the youngest Grand Prix world champion at the age of 21.

1962: T. C. Christensen sees a distinctive Norton motorcycle he nicknames the *Blue Behemoth.* The bike eventually becomes his double-engined *Hogslayer* and proceeds to dominate drag racing throughout most of the 1970s.

1962, December 10: The film *Lawrence of Arabia* premieres, and its opening sequence reconstructs the motorcycle ride which took the life of T. E. Lawrence.

1964, September: Steve McQueen joins four American riders—the first concerted U.S. effort—to compete in the International Six Days Trials on a Triumph TR6SC.

1967: After 47 years of continual improvements to his 1920 Indian Scout, Burt Munro achieves a one-way record of 190.07 miles per hour at the Bonneville Salt Flats.

1967, December 31: Evel Knievel unsuccessfully attempts to jump the fountains at Caesar's Palace in Las Vegas, which puts him in a coma for 29 days and launches his career as a motorcycle daredevil.

1968, July 8: Robert M. Pirsig and his son, Chris, embark on a roundtrip ride from Minneapolis to San Francisco on a 1964 Honda CB77 Superhawk, an experience that inspires the watershed book *Zen and the Art of Motorcycle Maintenance.*

1969, July 14: The film *Easy Rider* is released, eventually making *Captain America,* a raked and chopped Harley-Davidson Panhead, one of the most famous motorcycles of all time.

1969: Mert Lawwill wins the No. 1 plate in the AMA Grand National series. The following year he is featured—with Steve McQueen and Malcolm Smith—in the film *On Any Sunday.*

1970: Leo Payne sets a land speed record of 202.379 miles per hour on his *Turnip Eater,* a heavily modified Harley-Davidson Sportster.

1971: Dick Mann makes an unparalleled racing comeback, becoming the first rider ever to win the AMA Grand Slam, which includes mile, half-mile, short track, TT, and road racing events.

1972: Gifted American road racer Cal Rayborn shocks the world by winning three of the six Transatlantic Match Races on an outdated Harley-Davidson XR750.

1973, May 20: Popular Italian racer Renzo Pasolini loses control of his 250-cc Aermacchi at Monza's La Curva Grande, involving Jarno Saarinen in an accident that takes both of their lives.

1974: Phil Read wraps up MV Agusta's final 500-cc Grand Prix title, bringing the marque's total world championship tally to 37—a record that has yet to be broken.

1975, August 23: Kenny Roberts rides his notoriously overpowered Yamaha TZ750 past the two race leaders on the final lap to win the Indianapolis Mile.

1976: Evel Knievel's botched shark tank jump at the Chicago Amphitheater marks his final major public stunt.

1977, August 16: Elvis Aaron Presley dies at his Graceland estate in Memphis, Tennessee.

1979, June: At the age of 39, Mike Hailwood returns to the Isle of Man TT for the final time on a Ducati 950 F1 and finishes in fifth place, despite mechanical problems which force him to reattach the bike's battery in order to complete the final lap.

1980: Freddie Spencer beats Mike Hailwood's record, becoming the youngest Grand Prix world champion at the age of 21.

1980, October 10: Craig Vetter suffers severe injuries in an ultralight crash which lead him to abandon his ambitious *Mystery Ship* project. Though initial production is set at 200, only 10 bikes are produced.

1983: In the face of technologically superior competition, Wayne Rainey wins the 1983 Superbike Championship on his No. 60 Kawasaki GPz750.

1985: Freddie Spencer becomes the first and only person to win both 250-cc and 500-cc Grand Prix championships, while also winning all three divisions of Daytona Speed Week.

1991: John Britten's audacious V-1000 enters professional racing, scoring second- and third-place finishes against factory machines at Daytona's Battle of the Twins.

1992: Following three consecutive Grand Prix championships and on his way to a fourth, Wayne Rainey's racing career ends when he is injured in an accident that leaves him paralyzed from the chest down.

1992: At the age of 18, Colin Edwards wins five of nine AMA 250-cc National races during his first pro season, taking the championship and launching a career that eventually takes him to MotoGP.

1995, September 5: John Britten dies of melanoma shortly after his 45th birthday; the last of his 10 V-1000s are built after his death.

2004, March 4: Basketball legend Michael Jordan announces he will enter professional motorcycle racing by sponsoring Montez Stewart in the AMA Superstock and Supersport classes.

INDEX

Abbott, Ken, 128

Abrahams, Mort, 16, 17

Achorn, Mike and Margaret, 37, 38

Agostini, Giacomo, 134, 153–155, 159

Agusta, Domenico, 157

American Graffiti, 27

Andretti, Mario, 170

Angeli, Pier, 16

Ariel Square Four, 139

Bagnall, Bill, 148

Baker, Steve, 21, 22

Baldwin, Mike, 80

Barber, George, 135

Belland, Jim, 43

Bergstrom, Al, 43, 45

Betts, Bird, 120, 121, 124

Bimota KB1, 70

Bird, Larry, 129

Blob, The, 172, 173

Blue Behemoth, 27

Blue Bike, 136–141

BMW R60, 123, 164, 165

Branch, Jerry, 110

Brando, Marlon, 16, 102

Brelsford, Mark, 154

Britten V-1000, 106–111

Britten, John, 106–111

Brough Superior SS100, 94–99

Brough, George, 97, 99

Brown, Bruce, 44, 169

Brown, Gene, 122

Brown, George, 35

Bruce, Earl, 121

Bruton, Joe, 135

BSA 125, 113

BSA Gold Star, 52–57

Bullitt, 169

Captain America, 46–51

Carruthers, Kel, 22–25, 154

Carter, Marvin, 14, 19

Castine, Earl, 115

Chandler, Otis, 170–172

Christensen, T. C., 26–31

Clark, Gordy, 151

Clark, Kenny, 24, 25

Clark, Nobby, 135

Cleveland Fowler Four, 170, 171

Code, Keith, 69

Coleman, Dillard, 70, 71

Collins, Peter, 24

Condor 580-cc, 123–125

Covington, Jeff, 85

Craill, Shaun, 109

Cycle magazine, 56, 70, 71

CZ 125-cc, 13–16, 19

Damone, Vic, 16

Danielson, Frank, 169

Dean, James, 12–19

Dean, Winton, 19

Demott, Bill, 36

des Roches, Pierre, 69

Dickerson, Marty, 37, 38, 136–141, 143, 147, 149, 150

Draper, Mike, 116

Driven from Within, 130

Ducati

  950 F1, 134, 135

  998, 129

  Darmah, 108, 109

Dunaway, Faye, 169

Dunlop, Joey, 135

East of Eden, 15, 16

Edgar, John Jr., 39

Edgar, John Sr., 33, 36–39

Edwards, Colin, 84–87

Ekins, Bud, 120, 167–171

Elings, Virgil, 111

Elliot, Ron, 103

Emde, Don, 74, 76, 77

Enthusiast magazine, 101

Esposito, Joe, 103

Evans, Ted, 16, 19

Evans, Phil, 34

Fellman, James, 165

Flanders, Earl, 25, 148

Fonda, Peter, 46–48, 51

Foran, Ollie, 165

Forbes, Malcolm, 71

Free, Rollie, 14, 32–39, 138, 139, 143, 147–150

Geisler, David, 104

George, 96, 99, 94, 95, 97, 99

Giant, 17, 18

Granger, Gordon, 51

Great Escape, The, 167–169

Gregory, John, 29, 30

Gunter, Al, 54

Haggerty, Dan, 49, 51

Hailwood, Mike, 132–135, 153, 157

Halvorson, Tom, 86

Hardy, Ben, 48

Hargreaves, Burt, 97, 98

Harley-Davidson

  Electra-Glide, 101–105

  FLH Police Special, 120, 121

  Hummer, 101

  KR750, 40–45, 75

  Model K, 100, 101

  Panhead, 47, 51

  Sportster, 89, 90

  Sprint, 91

  XR750, 44, 72–77, 114, 116, 117, 152–155

  XRTT, 92

Harris, Herb, 38, 39, 137, 140

Hatfield, Tinker, 129, 130

Held, Mel, 36

Hemmings Motor News, 170

Hensley, Dean, 148, 151

Herring, Clifton, 129

Hocking, Rick, 22

Holden, Jake, 131

Honda

  350 Superhawk, 102

  600, 86

  750, 85

  CB77 Superhawk, 162–165

  Dream, 104, 105, 123

  GP motorcycle, 59–65, 80

  NSR-250, 65

  NSR-500, 65

  RC30, 86

Hopkins, Anthony, 151

Hopper, Dennis, 47, 48

Horiike, Satoru, 62

Hogslayer, 26–31

Huntzinger, Steve, 151

Iannucci, Robert, 56, 57

Iannuccilli, Michael, 111

Indian

  Chief, 172, 173

  Power Plus, 171

  Scout, 107, 143, 150, 151

  Sport Scout, 171, 172

  Warrior TT, 15

Irimajiri, Shoichiro, 59

Irving, Julius, 129

Irving, Phil, 34

Iscovich, Mario, 170

Ivy, Bill, 159

Jackson, Phil, 128

Jaguar XKSS, 172

John Edgar Lightning, 32–39, 138

Jones, Norman, 71

Jones, Ralph Neville, 98

Jordan, Michael, 126–131

Kanemoto, Erv, 59, 62

Kawasaki

  KZ1000, 69

  Superbike, 78–83

  Z1, 139, 140

  ZX-7, 85

Kazan, Elia, 15, 16

Keener, Corky, 24

Kelly, Sean, 169

Knaub, Jim, 71

Knievel, Evel, 112–117

Kosman, Sandy, 69

Kovacs, Laszlo, 48

Kretz, Ed, 37

Kuerbis, Tate, 129

Lawrence, Arnold, 99

Lawrence, T. E., 94–99

Lawson, Eddie, 63, 79, 80

Lawwill, Mert, 40–45, 154, 170

Le Mans, 170

Lean, David, 95

Liberace, 113

Life magazine, 138

Maely, Ken, 24, 25

Mann, Dick, 52–57

Manning, Denis, 75

Markel, Bart, 153, 154

Martin, Vince "Mickey," 137, 138, 140

Matchless GTO TT, 53–57

McEwan, Jason, 111

McQueen, Steve, 15, 166–173

Mercedes-Benz 300SL Gullwing, 121

Meyers, Bruce, 39

MG TD, 16

Minty, Barbara (McQueen), 170, 171

Moore, Peter, 130

Mork, Fred, 55, 57

Morrow, Carl, 91

Moss, Stirling, 148

Motor Cycle Weekly, 56, 76

Motorcyclist magazine, 148

Motorrad magazine, 71

Munro Special, 142–151

Munro, Burt, 140, 142–151

Murray, Boris, 29

MV Agusta, 133, 154, 156–161

Mystery Ship, 66–71

Neilson, Cook, 69

Norton 650, 27, 28

O'Brien, Dick, 74, 75

O'Toole, Peter, 95, 99

On Any Sunday, 44, 54, 169

Parham, John, 49, 51

Parriott, Sam, 139

Pasolini, Renzo, 152–155

Payne, Leo, 88–93

Perry, Geoff, 77

Petrali, Joe, 33, 34

Piazzano, Ted, 35

Pickrell, Ray, 74, 76

Picotte, Pascal, 110

Pierce, Sam, 150, 151

Pirsig, Chris, 162–165

Pirsig, Robert, 162–165

Porsche

  356 Super Speedster, 16

  550 Spyder, 13, 18

  908 Spyder, 170

Prentice, Archie, 143

Presley, Elvis, 100–105, 113

Presley, Priscilla, 103

Pridmore, Jason, 128, 130, 131

Pridmore, Reg, 69

Rainey, Wayne, 78–83

Rapp, Steve, 128, 130, 131

Ray, Nicholas, 16

Rayborn, Cal, 72–77, 154

Read, Phil, 154, 156–161

Rebel Without a Cause, 16, 17

Regazzoni, Clay, 135

Reiman, Roger, 114, 116

Road, The, 95, 96

Roberts, Kenny, 20–25, 59, 81, 86

Rossi, Valentino, 87, 126, 127

Roustabout, 102

Royal Enfield 500-cc, 15, 19

Saarinen, Jarno, 154, 155

Sarron, Christian, 63

Schilling, Phil, 69

Schoenewald, Daniel, 124, 172

Schwerma, Doug, 22–24

Scott, Gary, 22

Sedlack, George, 117

Seven Pillars of Wisdom, The, 97

Sheene, Barry, 59, 154, 161

Shenton, Stewart, 62

Simpson, Joe, 139

Smith, Dean, 129

Smith, George Sr., 90

Smith, Malcolm, 170

Smith, Mark, 129, 130

Spencer, Freddie, 58–65

Springsteen, Jay, 24

Stark, Bob, 172

Stern, David, 130

Stevens, George, 17, 18

Stewart, Montez, 127, 128, 131

Stroud, Andrew, 110

Sullivan, Ed, 102

Surtees, John, 34

Sutherland, Sylvia and John, 164, 165

Suzuki GSX-R 1000, 131

"Talk of the Town," 102

Tamburini, Massimo, 155

Thomas Crown Affair, The, 169

Thompson, David, 129

Thompson, Mickey, 151

Tompkins, Allen, 37

Triumph

  6T, 16

  Hurricane, 67, 70

  T110, 16

  Tiger 100, 137

  TR5 Trophy, 12, 13, 16–19

  TR6SC ISDT Works, 168, 169

Turnip Eater, 88–93

Vance, Terry, 31, 86

Vaughs, Cliff, 48

Vesco, Don, 37, 73

Vesco, John, 148

Vetter, Craig, 66–71

Vincent

  Black Lightning, 37, 139

  Black Shadow, 34, 37

  HRD, 33

  Rapide, 138, 147

Vincent, Philip, 33–35, 37, 138, 139

Von Dutch, 48, 118–125, 168

Wild One, The, 102

Williams, Ron, 135

Wilson, Mike, 89–93

Winslow, Marcus Jr., 14, 17, 19

Winslow, Marcus Sr., 13, 19

Wise, Steve, 80

Wood, Natalie, 16

Work, Bob, 21, 22

World's Fastest Indian, The, 151

Wright, Stephen, 24, 25, 170, 171

Wütherich, Rolf, 18

Wynn, Keenan, 123

Wynne, Steve, 134

Yamaha

  FZR1000, 85

  FZR400, 86

  R6, 128

  TZ250D, 84–87

  TZ750, 21–25, 59

  YZ250, 68

Zen and the Art of Motorcycle Maintenance, 163–165